Standoff in the Caribbean

ISBN: ISBN-13: 978-0615605708
ISBN-10: 0615605702

Cover Design: Ashley Spears
AES Graphics

Author photo: Rear Adm. Peter B. Booth, USN Ret.

Praise for
Standoff in the Caribbean

Standoff in the Caribbean is a fast-moving, gripping and historically correct rendering of the most perilous several weeks to our nation since the ending of World War Two. It's one that most readers will devour and pass along to their friends. Art Giberson, a prolific writer and master photojournalist, has done it again!

My compliments to Art Giberson for an engaging tale that is not only entertaining, but also a reminder of years gone by, of the tough nature of the Cold War, but also a glimpse into the toughness and personalities of life on the deck plates of a Navy destroyer. As he weaves the story, the sidebars into the pragmatics and importance of the Navy combat photographer are well-taken.

Standoff in the Caribbean is a most interesting literary addition for a talented and visionary author.

Rear Admiral Peter B. Booth, USN (Ret)

Other Books by Art Giberson

<u>Nonfiction</u>

Wall South

The Blue Ghost: The Ship That Couldn't be Sunk

Eyes of the Fleet: A History of Naval Photography

The Crazy Ones Shot Film

Century of War

Through the Viewfinder

The Mighty O: USS Oriskany CVA-34

The Pensacola Mill

War Stories

<u>Novels</u>

Photojournalist: Navy Combat Photographer

Anything but the Truth

In Memory of

Captain John B. McKamey, USN

Vietnam Prisoner of War 1965-1972
A dear friend and great Commanding Officer

Chapter 1

Barcelona, Spain
September 15, 1962

The crew of the American destroyer, *USS Kamey* stood at rigid attention in their starched white uniforms as the sleek man-of-war eased alongside the Barcelona pier under the watchful eye of Christopher Columbus, perched high atop a 131-foot tall tower pointing westward toward the New World.

On the bridge, the officer of the deck (OOD) stole a quick peek at the imposing statue through the open portside bridge door and proclaimed, to no one in particular: "Gentlemen we're looking at history. The Columbus Monument is built on the exact site where Columbus reported to Queen Isabella after his first voyage to the Americas."

"Now that's right nice to know lieutenant. But I'm a lot more interested in the site of the nearest bar," the boatswain's mate of the watch, a leathery-faced Irishman, sporting three hash marks, each representing four years of service, and the rating badge of a Boatswain's Mate Second Class, responded.

"Yeah," agreed the helmsmen, a tall skinny seaman from Wytheville, Virginia; "after a month at sea a tall cool one will taste mighty good. Course, it will taste a whole lot better if a few of Queen Isabella's female descendants are on hand to greet the best tin can crew in the Sixth Fleet," he chuckled.

"Pipe down!" growled the executive officer (XO), Lt. Commander. Paul Bolton. "This ain't no damn cruise ship. Knock off the lollygagging and pay attention to what you are doing."

"Lighten up XO," Commander. Ralph Feeney, *Kamey's* commanding officer, said softly. "After seven long months the crew deserves one final fling, a wakeup of sorts. Three more months and this old tin can will be in mothballs and we'll all have new duty stations."

"You know, skipper, I'm going to miss this old bucket of bolts. I've been aboard her going on five years now. I've spent my whole career in destroyers and I've got to say, *Kamey* has been the best. Yes sir, she been a mighty fine ship."

"That she has, Mr. Bolton that she has. I'll miss her too. *Kamey* was my first ship. Reported aboard as a green ensign right out of OCS, would never have dreamed that I would someday return as her final commanding officer. Yep, she's been a good ship alright — crewed by the best group of bluejackets that ever went to sea."

For several weeks before departing Mayport, Florida, *Kamey's* homeport, for a seven month Mediterranean deployment, rumors had been circulating that *Kamey* was to be decommissioned upon return to the States. It wasn't until midway through the deployment, however, that Captain Feeney received the official announcement that the proud old warship he commanded would be taken out of service upon return to Mayport.

Commissioned in April 1944, *Kamey* was immediately

[3]

dispatched to the Pacific. Two weeks after arriving on station near Okinawa, she was attacked by three Japanese kamikaze aircraft. *Kamey* gunners quickly shot down two of the enemy planes but the third managed to evade the wall of fire and crashed into the ship's port side forward of the bridge. A 500-kilogram bomb tore through several light bulkheads and exploded on the ship's starboard side, claiming the lives of fifteen crewmembers.

Although *Kamey* suffered extensive damage as a result of her first combat engagement, her gallant crew quickly extinguished the fires, made temporary repairs and sailed the wounded greyhound into Kerama Retto, a small island southwest of Okinawa. There, the destroyer received semi-permanent repairs and was sent back to the States for what was supposed to have been a three-month overhaul before returning to the war. *Kamey* was still undergoing repairs in a Navy shipyard when World War II ended.

Weighing in at around 2,200-tons, World War II-era destroyers, pound for pound, were reputedly the most heavily armed ships in the Navy. Numerous renovations during her 17 years of active service had changed *Kamey's* armament, but she still sported an awesome arsenal: three twin-turret 5-inch/38-caliber naval guns; four 21-inch torpedo tubes; two Mark-IX depth charge racks, anti-submarine rockets, 20 and 40 mm anti-aircraft guns and a helicopter flight deck and hanger. An awesome sight to be sure.

"Shift colors," Captain Feeney said to the boatswain's mate of the watch, who instantly pushed a button on the ship's 21-MC squawk box intercom and relayed the announcement throughout the ship. The Stars and Stripes, normally flown from the ship's mast while at sea, were stricken and at the same instant another U.S. flag was

[4]

hoisted on the ships fantail and a union jack was hoisted on the bow. A few minutes later the piercing trill of the boatswain's pipe preceded a second announcement:

"Double up all lines. Secure the sea and anchor detail."

USS Kamey ... after weeks at sea was once again resting securely alongside a pier and the crew's attention turned to liberty in one of Europe's most beautiful ports.

****

September 29, 1962

For the men of R Division, a part of *Kamey's* Engineering Department, this final port call at Barcelona was special. It was a farewell party of sorts. Prior to departing Mayport, the division officer, Ensign Randolph Harris, had suggested the establishment of a "slush fund." Each payday for the duration of the deployment; division personnel desiring to do so, donated five dollars to the fund which was to be used for a "going home party" in the last scheduled port call of the deployment. To ensure that all hands would be able to attend, the party would be held over a two day period. As a matter of courtesy Ensign Harris invited both the skipper and the XO.

The Captain declined the invitation but the XO, who had joined the Navy as an enlisted sailor and advanced through the ranks, thought it would be a good idea if he attended... just to make sure "nothing got out of hand." *USS Kamey*, despite her reputation as one of the fleet's top anti-submarine warships, also had a reputation as a "party ship."

At morning quarters the second day in port, R Division Leading Chief Jeff Curtis laid out the plans for the party.

"The division party will be held tonight and tomorrow night at Club Casa Juan, one of Barcelona's best night spots. Uniform will be service dress whites. The shindig will commence promptly at 1900. Mr. Harris has arranged for a bus to pick you up and return you to the ship after the party. The bus departs the pier at 1830. Anyone who isn't aboard will have to wait until tomorrow night."

"If someone misses the bus tonight and has the duty tomorrow night what does he do chief?" A sailor in the front rank asked.

"If you can't find a way to get there on your own you'll be shit out of luck. That's why this bash is scheduled over two nights. We're in a port and starboard duty status. Half of the crew has to be on board at all times. For your information," the chief continued, "the XO will probably be in attendance for at least one go-a-round, maybe both. So be on your best behavior. OK! Turn to."

Despite some minor scuffles for the attention of the few available ladies who had somehow managed to snag an invite to the party and numerous hangovers the morning after, both duty sections had behaved reasonably well and everyone had made it back to the ship on time and was ready to set sail for Mayport.

****

With the conclusion of the five-day Barcelona port call, *USS Kamey* cast off her lines and set sail for Golfo Di Palmas where the destroyer *USS Bristol* was standing by to relieve her. After a long, grueling seven month deployment, including six weeks in the Red Sea, the crew's thoughts shifted from near constant anti-submarine patrol and plane guard duty to home, family and friends.

The destroyer's impending decommissioning and future duty assignments also gave Captain Feeney and the crew plenty to think about. Many of the 230-plus man crew had already received orders to other ships, shore stations or technical schools and several others were due to be discharged or retire.

Commander Feeney had been recommended for promotion to Captain and was scheduled to take command of the heavy cruiser *USS Boston.*

Prior to the commencement of the current deployment Lt. Commander Paul Bolton, after 29 years of naval service, had decided he had been at sea long enough and was scheduled to retire in early November.

Ship decommissionings and crew reassignments are a part of Navy life. Some would miss their old ship and others couldn't wait to get off of the *Kamey* and find new adventures elsewhere. Still, most agreed, it would be a sad day when the *Kamey*, a combat veteran of World War II and Korea was taken out of service. Love her or hate her, *USS Kamey* would forever be a part of every crewmember's life. As far as most sailors are concerned the best ship they ever served in is the one they are leaving and the one they are being reassigned to.

As *Kamey* sailed through the Strait of Gibraltar into the Atlantic, Captain Feeney's focus shifted from patrol operations to the Atlantic Ocean sea state.

Hurricane season, at its peak during the months of September and October, was a major concern for sea captains of any size vessel venturing into the Atlantic at this time of the year.

Far from the Strait of Gibraltar; the commander of Naval Base Guantanamo Bay, Cuban, was agonizing over a problem of far greater significance. Intelligence reports

were showing sizable increases in the number of Soviet
Bloc ships bound for Cuban ports. According to the intelligence, an average of 14 Soviet dry-cargo ships per
month had called at Cuban ports during the first six
months of 1962. In August that figure more than dou-
bled.

Given the state of the Cuban economy an increase in the
number of ships bringing food and other humanitarian
necessities to the island nation wasn't that surprising; but
the presence of Soviet technicians and military personnel, construction of large launch complexes and the ex-
tension of airstrips to accommodate high-performance
aircraft, possibly for offensive action against the United
States, caused the Navy to be placed on heighted alert
status. Even more alarming were reports of Soviet submarines docked at the Cuban port of Bahia de Nipe.

To make matters worse a Naval Air Station, Key West-
based S2F anti-submarine aircraft, flown by a reserve
naval officer on active duty for training, made contact
with what was believed to have been a Soviet submarine,
near the mouth of Havana harbor.

"Y'all sure 'bout that contact," the pilot, Lieutenant
Commander Tex Atkinson, a tall, willowy Texan, asked
the sonar operator.

"Aye, aye, skipper. I have a solid blip on the screen.
No visual yet, but I know for certain it's not a whale.
Has to be a sub; he's 'bout a mile behind us."

"Maintain contact, I'm coming about."

Quickly reversing course Atkinson flew low over the
point of contact. "What do you have sonar?"

"I've lost him sir. The moment you turned, the blip disappeared from the screen."

Despite the fact that it was a clear calm day with hardly any wind on the surface, the only visible sign of anything having been there only moments before was a small oil slick ... certainly not unusual in an area with considerable boat and ship traffic.

"Keep searching sonar, I'll make another pass," Atkinson said turning toward the mouth of the harbor.

"Contact!" the sonar operator suddenly cried out as a blip popped upon the screen. "Standing by to drop sonobuoys sir," the sonar tech informed Atkinson.

"Negative sonar: Hold the sonobuoys"

Atkinson, a seasoned naval aviator who had flown combat missions from the carriers *USS Princeton* and *USS Boxer* during the Korean War was sensitive to the possible political ramifications of putting listening devices in Cuban waters, quickly dictated a classified message for transmission back to Key West.

Returning to base, Atkinson was directed to taxi to the base of the control tower, where a Navy van was standing by to take him and his crew to the headquarters building for a debriefing with the admiral.

"Commander ain't it a bit unusual for a flag debriefing of a routine flight?" the co-pilot asked.

"Yeah, what do you think is going on Mr. Atkinson," the sonar tech inquired.

"I have no idea guys. I guess we're about to find out though.

Without the slightest hint of the seriousness of the situation the admiral questioned the crew, particularly the two enlisted technicians one-by-one, about what they had observed. After about thirty minutes the admiral complimented the four-man S2F crew on being observant and dismissed them without any mention of the magnitude of what was happening.

Chapter 2

Mayport, Florida

Normally late September, early October is the worst possible time to be sailing across the Atlantic. But to the delight of *Kamey's* crew the weather couldn't have been better. It was like sailing on glass; beautiful sunny days and perfectly calm seas. Unfortunately, the great weather actually worked against them. *Kamey* was scheduled to return to Mayport on 10 October. Plans for the official welcome home ceremony had been made, families had been notified of the ship's arrival time, and everything was in place, including contingency plans for a weather related late arrival. An early arrival, however, was totally out of the question which meant that when *Kamey* arrived off Mayport on October 7 she was denied permission to enter port.

After three days of streaming in circles, mindless war games, and cleaning the ship from stem to stern for the umpteenth time, the veteran old warship finally steamed into Mayport, right on schedule, where families and friends waited on the pier.

Liberty was granted the moment the ship was tied up. The brown baggers (crewmembers with family residing in the area) left the ship first, followed by those who had received orders or transfer. Within an hour of docking the only crewmembers remaining on board were mostly those poor unfortunate souls in the duty section and those just securing from the sea and anchor detail.

BM2 Donald Patton, poked his head through the open water tight door of the R Division berthing compartment and yelled, "Yo Andy, y'all in here?"

"Yo Boats, be right there," a raspy voice answered from behind a bank of lockers. "Just need to splash on a dab of Old Spice. Gotta smell good for the ladies you know."

"Well, la-de-da! Don't y'all look pretty? And you're right about that Old Spice. It sho 'nuff makes you smell. Course if you would go topside every now and then for a dab of fresh air you wouldn't need Old Spice."

"Ah, stuff it deck ape. What the hell does a boatswain's mate know about anything? You're like seagulls. All you do is flutter about and squeak."

Though one would never know it by listening to their nattering, Donald Patton and Andy Warden were actually the best of friends. Both had a little more than 12 years in the Navy. Both were rated by their superiors as outstanding sailors who excelled in their respective military specialties; and, both were notorious for getting into trouble when ashore, which had, on more than one occasion, resulted in the loss of a stripe or two.

"What say we stop by the Acey-Ducy Club for a quick one before going into Jacksonville," Patton suggested.

"Suits me just fine boats, let's go."

"Where the hell did all this stuff come from?" the two asked in unison as they departed the destroyer piers.

Military equipment: tanks, armored personnel carriers, jeeps, trucks and heavy artillery pieces were scattered about all over the place.

"Man I've never seen anything like this," Warden said, "how 'bout you?"

"Nope, me neither. What do think is going on?"

"I don't know. I guess maybe we can find out something when we get to the club."

"Yeah, maybe."

Acey-Ducy Clubs, as opposed to other Navy service clubs were designed exclusively for Navy first and second class petty officers and their Marine Corps counterparts, sergeants and staff sergeants.

The Mayport Acey-Ducy Club would have been a private entrepreneur's dream. Set on top of a hill overlooking the waterfront, the club, at any given time catered to the crews of an aircraft carrier, a dozen or more destroyers, a destroyer tender, a couple of cruisers, supply and ammo ships, tankers and numerous visiting warships from several countries. On any night the Mayport Acey-Ducy Club could count on entertaining several hundred Sailors and Marines and their guests.

"Welcome home guys!" Marty the bartender, a robust, silver-haired navy retiree shouted, instantly recognizing Warden and Patton. "Business has been slack without my two favorite customers. Whatta you have... your usual?"

"Say, Marty, what's the deal with all the heavy military stuff? Are we preparing for some kind of an attack?"

Patton asked the bartender, as he placed two Budweisers on the bar in front of them.

"Can't really say Boats. That stuff started arriving about a week ago...mostly army stuff. There's been some talk about some sort of exercise."

During the course of the evening, the two *Kamey* blue-jackets learned that a military exercise code named "Ortsac" was about to begin at Vieques Island off Puerto Rico. The exercise would include air, naval and land forces. Operations of this sort weren't unusual and Patton and Warden felt pretty certain that because *Kamey* had just returned from an overseas deployment, their ship wouldn't be involved. But the unusual amount and type of equipment continued to be the major topic as other sailors and a few marines joined Patton and Warden.

"What the hell does Ortsac mean anyway?" a sailor from the Mayport based carrier *USS Shangri-La*, asked.

"Who knows how the brass comes up with names for military exercises," Patton answered. "I bet they have a team of high-paid civilians in the Pentagon whose only job is to dream up stupid names for military operations."

"Hey, wait a minute!" the *Shangri-La* sailor, a first class signalman, who had been doodling on a napkin said. "Look at this, O-R-T-S-A-C. That's Castro... spelled backwards."

"What! No way," Warden exclaimed pulling a pen from his pocket. "Well I'll be damned. It does spell Castro."

"Do you think there's a connection?" Patton asked.

"Nah," just a coincidence," another sailor said, taking a swig of his Black Label.

"Yeah, you're probably right. Why would the Navy name anything after a commie dictator, spelled backwards or any other way?"

"Yeah, purely coincidental," everyone at the table agreed.

****

RINGGGGG! RINGGGGG!

"Lt. Commander Paul Bolton," the *Kamey* XO said sleepily.

"XO, this is the Captain We need to round up the crew and get them back to the ship, ASAP!"

"Aye, Aye Sir, but what, may I ask, is going on? You know of course that more than half of the crew are either on leave or in transit to new duty stations and more than likely are scattered all over the country by now."

"I know it's going to be a big headache, Paul, but it has to be done. We've been placed on DEFCON-3 and ordered to standby to get underway on an hour's notice."

"DEFCON THREE! No shit? That's just two steps from an imminent attack alert Captain"

"I'm very much aware of what it means Mr. Bolton. That's why we need to get as many as we can back on board as quickly as possible. ComNavForJax (Commander Naval Forces Jacksonville) has asked the Jacksonville Police and Duval County Sheriff's Department to assist in rounding up naval personnel and getting them back to their commands. I'll see you aboard the ship in 45 minutes. Oh, and Paul, I want an all hands muster report as soon as possible."

"What's wrong," Bolton's wife Irene, asked as he stumbled out of bed.

"I don't know. That was the Captain He said something about us being placed on a heighted alert. Gotta get back to the ship."

"Honey, its 4 a.m.!"

"I know sweetheart, but duty calls. Could you make me a cup of coffee, please, while I make a couple quick phone calls?"

"Of course, want me to start your shower?"

"Don't have time. I'll get a shower aboard ship."

The XO's first call was to the ship's personnel officer. "Good morning, Sir," Ensign John Miller sleepily answered a few minutes later.

"Mr. Miller, do you have addresses and phone numbers for all of our people who went on leave and liberty yesterday?"

"Yes sir. Is there anyone in particular you need to contact sir?"

"All of them. We need to get everyone back to the ship as quickly as possible. That includes those with orders for transfer and separation from service. Start with the people residing in the Mayport/Jacksonville area."

Aye, aye sir. But what should I do if the men who left the area haven't arrived at their destinations yet?"

"Leave a message for them to contact the ship ASAP."

"I'm on it sir."

****

Tap...tap...tap

"Wha...what is it?" Patten moaned as he groggily opened his eyes and looked into the face of a Duval County Sheriff's deputy.

The deputy shined his flashlight into the car, momentary focusing the beam on each of the four bewildered sailors suffering from a long night of overindulgence.

"Rise and shine fellows," the deputy said, motioning for the car window to be rolled down. "The Gator Bowl parking lot ain't a camp site you know. What are you do-ing here anyway?"

"We're sorry, officer," the *Shangri-La* first class petty officer said, "we were celebrating the homecoming of the *USS Kamey* and I guess we had a little too much to drink. Decided to pull in here and sleep it off rather than try and drive back to the base."

"That was the smart thing to do fellows. I appreciate that. Now, if you're sober enough to drive you need to get back to your ships immediately."

"What's going on?"

"Some sort of an emergency recall. The Navy has asked the local police to help round you guys up. If you don't think you can drive safely I will take you back," the deputy offered.

"No that's alright. I think we're OK now."

"Fine, now if I can get your names and the ships you're assigned to."

"I'm Signalman First Class Joseph Walker, *USS Shangri-La*. This," he said pointing to Patten, "is Boatswain's Mate Second Class Donald Patton, *USS Kamey*. That's Shipfitter Second Class Andy Warden; *USS Kamey* and Quartermaster Second Class Keith Bowlighter; *USS Shangri-La,* in the back seat."

"OK fellows. Drive carefully and good luck."

"Can you believe this?" Walker said turning left off Mayport Road onto Perimeter Road, the main drag to the naval station."We don't have this much traffic during normal rush hour."

"Yeah." said Patten, "I know ComNavForJax is notorious for drills, but this is ridiculous, looks like every ship at Mayport is being recalled. Wonder if it has anything to with all that ground-pounder crap scattered all over the base?"

"I don't know if there is any connection or not, but I do know we'll never going find a parking spot anywhere near the ship with this mess," Walker said after slowly managing to get through the naval station gate, "so if it's OK with you guys I am grabbing the first spot I can find and we'll hike the rest of the way."

"Seeing as how you're driving, it doesn't look as though we have a hell of a lot to say about it, now does it Airedale," Petty Officer Warden said jokingly, referring to the nickname destroyer sailors often use when making reference to aircraft carrier sailors.

"Nope, you sure don't and we start hiking it from right here," Walker said wheeling into a narrow vacant spot on the side of the road.

"Thank it's safe to leave your car here," Bowlighter queried, "ain't you afraid it will be towed?"

"It probably will be Keith, but that's a hell of a sight better than the ramifications of missing ship if we do have to get underway. I'll check with legal as soon as I get aboard. Surely we'll be cut a little slack under the circumstances."

****

USS *Kamey* Wardroom

"Now hear this, now hear this! All officers and chief petty officers, not actually on watch, muster in the wardroom."

"Well now, it looks like we might finally get a hint as to what's going on," said *Kamey* operations officer Lieutenant Jack Winslow.

"I just hope it doesn't involve getting underway, responded visibly concerned engineering officer, Lieutenant (junior grade) Robert Dollar. "More than half of my snipes are either on leave or in route to service schools.

"We're all in the same boat, no pun intended," laughed Lieutenant (junior grade) Frank Campbell. "Gunnery doesn't have enough people to swab the decks, let alone operate the weapons systems. What do think chief?"

"I have a bad feeling about this," Chief Boatswain's Mate Larry Sanders answered. "The last time I was called back to a ship in the middle of the night, North Korea had just crossed the 38th Parallel."

Lt. Commander. Paul Bolton stood just inside the wardroom door holding a steaming coffee mug. "Don't worry about seating arrangements," he barked, "just grab a seat, Captain's on his way."

"Attention on deck!" Bolton snapped a minute or so later as Captain Feeney entered the room.

"At ease, gentlemen. Is this everyone XO?" Captain Feeney asked looking at the sparsely filled room.

"Yes sir, I have the muster report right here Captain We have only seven of our fifteen officers on board and four of the eight chiefs."

"OK. I want a report from each department. Then I'll brief you on what I know. Let's start with communications."

"Sir, the Communications Department has thirteen men, including the communications officer, and one chief on leave."

"Engineering."

"We're in pretty bad shape Captain," Lt. (jg) Dollar reported, "Both fire room supervisors are on leave but fortunately I have several excellent first and second class petty officers who can handle the task. The R Division Chief, ENC Curtis, can oversee B Division as well as his own people if necessary. The biggest problem sir, will be finding enough qualified watch standers. R Division has some very good men; damage controlmen, electrician's mates and shipfitters. But none of them are qualified to stand fire or engine room watches."

"What's the bottom line Mr. Dollar?"

"Out of the sixty-seven men assigned to Engineering, thirty-six are off the ship. Which means, sir, we are way undermanned."

"Extend the watch sections as you deem necessary, Mr. Dollar. We'll have to make do with what we have."

The Wardroom reports quickly confirmed what Captain Feeney had already guessed. If the *USS Kamey* was ordered to get underway she would be manned with only a bare skeleton crew. Certainly not the ideal situation, but he was equally confident, that if the order came, *Kamey* would be equal to the task.

"How are you doing on getting our missing crewmembers back, Ens. Miller," the XO asked.

"We've made contact with about sixty percent of them sir, that includes those detached from the ship, but still in a leave status. All transfers, schools, separations from service and retirements have been put on hold. I don't know how we'll get those men back on board though if the ship gets underway, sir."

"Neither do I Mr. Miller, neither do I," the Captain

chimed in. "That's a whole different kittle of fish. We'll just have to wait and see what happens."

"I know everyone is anxious to know what's going on. Unfortunately, I don't have a lot to share with you. I will bring you up to date the best I can, however.

"According to a 'Commander's Eyes Only', message I received early this morning, the president, based on aerial photographs taken by an Air Force U-2 reconnaissance aircraft, and intelligence sources on the ground in Cuba, has placed the armed forces on readiness condition three... DEFCON-3. That, gentlemen, means all branches of the armed forces must be ready to respond within 24 hours. As far as the Navy is concerned, all East Coast ships have been put on notice to prepare to get under way on an hour's notice, or sooner. Now you know as much as I do about what going on," Captain Feeney said. "Questions?"

Nearly every hand in the room reached for the overhead everyone trying to speak at once.

"Hold it down," the Captain shouted. "One at a time, please. XO," he said pointing to the executive officer.

"Captain, just what did these photographs show?"

"I can't go into that right now, so let it suffice to say that troops from several Soviet Bloc nations have been recorded disembarking from ships at various Cuban ports. It isn't clear what their intentions are, but the Secretary of Defense and the Joint Chiefs are deeply concerned."

"What can we tell the men, sir?"

"At this point there's not much you can tell them XO.

Everything I have told you is classified and is not to be repeated outside this room. Just tell them that we have been placed on high alert and we're standing by for orders to get underway. I know that's certainly not going to stop the scuttlebutt, but it's the best we have at the moment. John," Feeney said to the personnel officer "keep the XO advised about returning personnel. That's all gentlemen. Carry on."

****

For the Defense Department, the calamity had actually began a few days earlier when high-flying reconnaissance aircraft took photographs revealing several heavy construction projects underway on the island of Cuba. After careful examination of the photographs by military and defense photo interpretation experts, President John F. Kennedy was informed by his advisors that the photographs revealed the construction of what were believed to be missile installations.

After seven days of guarded and intense debate within the upper echelons of government, the president decided it was time for immediate action.

Chapter 3

White House Situation Room; 24 hours earlier

The President and Joint Chiefs of Staff were in full agreement that the drama unfolding in Cuba had to be handled quickly and effectively. Fortunately steps were already in play, thanks to previously scheduled naval exercises which had placed a substantial number of warships throughout the Caribbean and South Atlantic basin.

"The clandestine introduction of offensive weapons of mass destruction into Cuba by the Soviets constitutes a direct threat to the peace and security of the Western Hemisphere," Secretary of Defense Robert McNamara told the president at a quickly assembled gathering of the president's key advisors.

"I'm in full agreement, Bob, but what options do we have?" the commander-in-chief asked.

"Mr. President, I have placed the Air Force on full alert. You give the order Sir and the problem will be solved," the Air Force Chief of Staff said confidently.

"There is no question, Mr. President, that those U-2 photographs clearly show that the Cuban and Soviet governments are up to something," volunteered Lt. General Joseph Carroll, Director of the Defense Intelligence Agency. "We have undeniable photographic evidence that a massive military buildup is taking place in Cuba. Just this morning, an Air Force U-2 revealed the construction of what appears to be Soviet SSA Sandal medium-range ballistic missile sites in Cuba. Those missiles, Mr. President, have a range of one thousand, twenty nautical miles. We believe that as many as forty-two of them, equipped with two; perhaps three-megaton warheads have been deployed to Cuba. The U-2 flight also found SS-5 Skean intermediate-range ballistic missiles with a range of twenty two hundred nautical miles."

"What about Soviet naval forces, Admiral?" The president asked the Chief of Naval Operations, Admiral George W. Anderson, "Do they have any warships in Cuba?"

"Sir, according to intelligence we've received from our sources in Moscow, we know that four diesel-powered submarines assigned to the Soviet Northern Fleet departed the Polyarny Naval Base three days ago and appear to be headed for the Atlantic. Our long range antisubmarine patrol squadrons have been placed on full alert. If they are headed for Cuba, we'll find them. Other than an old destroyer or two there are, to the best of our knowledge, no other Soviet warships in Cuban.

While the President and his civilian and military assistants considered the courses open to the United States, they felt that it was imperative that the public not be unnecessarily alarmed.

"Has any of this leaked to the media?" the President asked.

"It's hard to say Sir. Rumors of increased military activities have started to circulate," Press Secretary Pierre Salinger answered. "They're mostly based on the unannounced departure of warships from ports all along the East Coast. And there have been questions from governors and mayors in the affected areas."

"I can certainly understand their concern, but it's vital that maximum secrecy be maintained until our course of action is firmly determined, and we can't determine that until we learn more about what the Soviets are actually building in Cuba. The U-2 photos have to be verified. The question is — how can we do that?" The President asked.

"The Navy and the Naval Photographic Interpretation Center have been testing a new Navy developed aerial camera which has recorded some remarkable reconnaissance photos during low-level reconnaissance flights by the Navy's RF-8A Photo Crusader aircraft," General Carroll said. "Perhaps they can be used for a low level, high speed reconnaissance flight over the island."

"Can we do this Admiral?" SecDef asked the CNO.

"Yes Sir, I believe we can. High-flying U-2s can take only one to two frames a minute, but an RF-8, equipped with the Navy's new KA-45 and KA-46 camera systems, can take several frames a second flying at 5,000 feet at a speed of 600 knots. If everything works as advertised it will provide far greater coverage than we can get from the U-2s. Unfortunately, flying at such a low altitude, Mr. President, will put the aircraft and pilots at great risk. But yes sir, the Navy can do the job."

Okay! Let's do it. Oh, and Admiral, I would prefer that the pilots be volunteers."

"Pierre," the president said to his Press Secretary, "If the media starts asking questions tell them that the armed forces have to be prepared for any eventuality and that this is merely part of a previously scheduled naval amphibious exercise in the Caribbean and South Atlantic. And, just to keep the wolves at bay, say these exercises actually started earlier in the year and includes a gradual buildup of air defenses in the southeastern United States. And, Pierre, for appearances, let's keep my normal travel schedule on track as much as possible."

"Bob," the president asked Secretary McNamara, "What is the Pentagon's posture on all of this?"

"Mr. President the entire defense establishment has been placed on alert status. The Army, Navy, Marine Corps and Air Force are ready for any emergency and the command organization is in place. CINCLANT (Commander in Chief, Atlantic), will provide unified command as well as retain control of all naval components involved in tactical operations.

"The responsibility for Army and Air Force components has been assigned to the Continental Army Command and the Tactical Air Command. The Strategic Air Command has dispersed its bombers and placed all aircraft on an upgraded alert and ready for takeoff within fifteen minutes. Our Intercontinental Ballistic Missile crews have assumed a comparable alert status. I defer the status of the Navy to Admiral Anderson."

"Sir, Commander Second Fleet," the Admiral said, "is embarked aboard the cruiser *Newport News* off Nova Scotia. The attack carriers *Enterprise* and *Independence* are standing by in the Caribbean and the anti-submarine carriers: *Wasp*, *Essex* and *Lake Champlain* are currently in port in the Boston/Newport area. *Intrepid* is at sea off

New York conducting routine operations, *Randolph* is in port at Norfolk. The guided missile cruiser *Canberra* is in the Caribbean along with six destroyers and an amphibious ship. The ASW carrier *Shangri-La,* and seven destroyers, one of which the *USS Kamey,* has just returned from a seven-month Mediterranean deployment and is fully combat ready, are in Mayport. All six U.S. Polaris ballistic missile submarines based at Holy Loch, Scotland, have been ordered to pre-assigned stations at sea."

"Our air defense forces," the Air Force Chief of Staff interjected without waiting to be asked, "are equally ready for any emergency Mr. President. Fighter interceptors and Hawk and Nike-Hercules missile battalions have been moved to the southeast to supplement local air defense forces. Interceptor units are on a 10-minute alert status. Like I said before Mr. President, you give the order and any problem we may have with the Cubans, or their Soviet handlers, will be solved."

"Thank you general, I will keep that in mind," the President said, rolling his eyes and turning his attention back to the Chief of Naval Operations. "Admiral when can your photo people get me some pictures?"

"Navy and Marine photo squadrons are standing by and ready for flight on your command, Sir."

"Thank you Admiral. Dean, what do you think Castro hopes to gain by letting the Soviets place missiles in Cuban," the President asked Secretary of State Dean Rusk.

"Well, Sir, Castro has been on edge ever since the failed CIA led Bay of Pigs invasion earlier this year. He is convinced that the United States is planning a second attack and he is willing to accept offers from anyone to help defend the island. I have no doubt that Khrushchev made him an offer that he felt he couldn't refuse."

****

CINCLANT Headquarters
Norfolk, Virginia

"Gentlemen!" the Commander–in-Chief Atlantic, greeted his visitors, Director of the Photographic Division of the Bureau of Weapons and Director of the Office of Photography and Reconnaissance. "CNO has a very special assignment for you… one that could decide whether or not we go to war."

The two senior naval photo officers looked at each other; confusion plainly visibly on their faces. "How do we manage that, Sir?" the Photo Division Director asked.

"I want you to go to Jacksonville for a conference with the commanding officer of VFP-62. I need to know if they have the men, machines and materials to handle sustained high-speed low-level reconnaissance flights over Cuba. Air Force U-2 reconnaissance flights have revealed what appear to be SAM missile sites in Cuba, but it's hard to confirm that from the U-2 images. That's where we come in. By the way, this is a top secret operation code named Project Blue Moon."

****

NAS Cecil Field
Jacksonville, Florida

Although the RF-8A Photo Crusader had been in service
for five years, Project Blue Moon would be its first actual operational test. The KA-45 and KA-46 70mm cameras used by the Navy and Marine Photo Fighter Squadrons, through technically still in the testing stage had, to
the delight of the aerial photo reconnaissance community, revealed promising results in both military exercises
and actual low-level photo reconnaissance flights.

"Good morning, gentlemen," Commander. Rob Johnson,
commanding officer of VFP-62, said as his two Washington visitors entered the small squadron office. "I understand you have a special mission for Fightin' Photo."

"You could say that commander. The State Department
has asked the Navy to fly a high-speed low-level recon
mission over Cuba and CINCLANT wants to make sure
your new cameras are up to the task."

"We have encountered a few problems with mounting
the KA-45 and 46 cameras in the RF-8A," Johnson told
his visitors. "But for the most part our maintenance people have everything under control. My biggest concern
isn't the skill of my pilots and crews, but a lack of high-
speed film processing equipment."

"Why is that, commander? Isn't the squadron equipped
with the new Eastman Kodak Versamat processing machines?"

"No Sir. I have repeatedly requested them, but to no
avail. But I can assure you Fightin' Photo is more than
capable of handling the job and the fleet photo lab here

at Cecil is a first rate processing facility capable of handling all types of film processing."

"Good. That's what we were hoping to hear," the BuWeps Photo director said. "One final thing commander, CINCLANT has directed that you assign two of your birds and two of your best pilots to NAS Key West to await further orders. Oh, and by the way commander, you will be getting your processing machines."

Two days later an Eastman Kodak technician arrived at the Fleet Air Photo Lab with two, still in the crate, Kodak Versamat film processing machines.

<u>Chapter 4</u>

USS Kamey

The high-pitched warble of a boatswain's pipe, followed instantly by the squawk of the 1-mc, brought all hands to full alert. "Now hear this. Now hear this. Liberty will commence for all hands not on watch at 1300. Liberty will expire onboard at 0600."

"Would somebody please tell what the hell is going on?" snapped Chief Boiler Tender Maxwell Dunlap who had just been returned to *USS Kamey* by the Shore Patrol.

"The cops come banging on my door up in Savannah at 0400 and tell me I have to get back to the ship. Now I'm free to go back on liberty! What the hell is going on Mr. Mann?" the chief demanded of the OOD.

"Chief, your guess is as good as mine. Some sort of a drill I guess."

"I'll get to the bottom of this crap. Is the XO aboard?"

"Well yeah, but, but you can't just barge in on the XO," the young ensign whimpered as the grizzled old chief hustled off towards the executive officer's state room.

"Can he do that?" the ensign asked the Junior Officer of the Deck, a second class petty officer.

[32]

"Sir, Chief Dunlap can do pretty much anything he sets his mind to. But if you want to try and stop him ... go right ahead."

The confused ensign looked first at the JOOD, then the departing broad backside of the chief and said in a low groan, "I guess he knows what he's doing."

I wonder how long it will take him to learn the ropes about who really runs this man's Navy," the duty messenger sniggered under his breath.

"Ah, give the ensign a break," the JOOD said softy so as not be overheard by the OOD. "He's just a few months out of the academy, he'll learn."

"Come on in Chief," Lt. Commander Bolton said looking up from a stack of papers on his desk.

"What's going on XO? I'm shanghaied out of my bed at Oh dark thirty, break every damn speed law in two states trying to get back to the ship ... just to be told that liberty will commence at 1300!"

"Don't get your skivvies in a knot, Max. We're caught between the devil and the deep blue sea with this one. There are all sorts of scuttlebutt floating about, but I can tell you that every ship in the Atlantic Fleet has been placed on full alert and ordered to stand by to get underway on a one hour notice. About an hour ago, Destroyer Squadron Sixteen authorized restricted liberty for the immediate Jacksonville area. The only other thing I can tell you is that I'm damn glad you're back on board. The thought of going to sea without the Navy's best damn boiler tender on board is downright scary."

"Paul, we've known each other way too long to start whistling into the wind now," the chief said breaking military protocol by referring to the executive officer by his given name. "So give me some slack on this."

The chief and XO had grown up in the same small town in Eastern Tennessee, had joined the Navy together and had served together on three different destroyers as enlisted men before Bolton had been commissioned.

"You're absolutely right, Max. Okay, here's what I know. Aerial photographs taken by Air Force U-2 aircraft show what is believed to be ICBM sites being constructed in Cuba. The Pentagon believes the Soviets may be planning an attack on the United States. So just to be on the safe side, we've been placed on DEFCON-3. Max, what I have just told you is top secret. When more information is released I will brief you and the other chiefs. I wish I could tell you more, but we just don't have anything. For what it's worth, Max, the Captain is just as frustrated as you are."

"Thanks XO, I owe you. Now if you will excuse me I'll get the fire rooms ready to make steam."

****

0800 October 11

"All hands fall in for muster," a harsh voice commanded over the 1-mc speakers. "Division officers make morning reports to the XO on the bridge."

As sailors throughout the ship assembled at their assigned muster stations, chiefs and leading petty officers called out their names. When each man had responded the report was then given to the division officer.

[34]

When all divisions had reported the crew was dismissed with the crisp command ... "Turn to! Commence ship's work."

Much to the skipper's dismay the morning reports brought a mixture of good and bad news. Thirty-two crewmen who had departed the ship for other assignments or who had been on leave, had returned to the *Kamey*. A near equal number had not yet been located which meant that *Kamey* would most likely be putting to sea with only a fraction of her normal at sea complement.

"Mr. Harris, I need gun mounts for an M60 machine gun erected on each side of the bridge. Have one of your shipfitters check with the gunnery officer for instructions as to where the mounts are to be located," the Captain instructed the R Division officer.

"If there is anything that needs to be done ashore, let's get it done ASAP. We'll probably be getting underway in a couple of hours. That's all," the Captain said ending the morning reports meeting, "Let's get the ship ready to go to sea."

****

NAS Key West, 0900

A lone VFP-62 Crusader lifted off the runway at NAS Key West, joined up with two other RF-8s from Jacksonville over the Florida Straits and set course for Cuba, 90 miles away. Project Blue Moon had begun.

Rather than return to Key West after their high speed photo venture the three photo birds returned to their home base at NAS Cecil Field. The planes had barely touched down before waiting Navy photographers re-moved the film canisters and rushed them to the Fleet Photo Lab for processing with the newly installed Kodak Versamat film processing machines.

****

USS Kamey 1700

"It's gonna be a bitch if we have to get underway with half the crew missing, but it sure makes the chow line a lot shorter," Shipfitter Second Class Andy Warden said cheerfully, noting the small number of men in the evening chow line.

"Yeah, like they say there's always a silver lining even in the darkest cloud," DC3 Frank Anderson, the only damage controlman assigned to *Kamey* said as he set his metal food tray on the mess table opposite *Kamey's* senior radioman RM1 Jeff Nagle.

"So, what's the word up in CIC Nag?" he asked.

"Lots a chatter Andy, but nothing we can bite into. I will tell you this though, if something don't happen pretty damn soon we're gonna have a mutiny up there. We're working four on two off. I don't know how much of this we can handle before we all start going bonkers."

"I don't know what y'all got to bitch about. At least y'all got air conditioning in the spook cave," BT2 Charlie Pate moaned. "Y'all should try standing a watch down in the hole where it's hotter than an Alabama July. Hell I'll swap with you any time you say the word."

"Well now, I do appreciate that Petty Officer Pate," Nagle replied sarcastically, "but as I see it, there are a couple of problems with your offer: First, I don't think the ship's evaporators could make enough fresh water to wash the dirt and grime off you snipes, and second, science would have to find a way to raise your IQ at least as high as a nit's ass before you could even get through the door of CIC."

"How would you like your tweedy bird ass kicked?" Pate screamed, grabbing the radioman's shirt.

"Knock it off you two! Or I'll have both your asses up on deck chipping paint," Chief Boatswain's Mate Sanders, passing through the crews mess en route to the CPO quarters, snapped.

"Hey, no problem, chief, we were just joking around. Right, Pate?" Nagle said, playfully tapping the boiler tender on the shoulder.

"Yeah right, Boats, we were just horsing around," Pate agreed.

"Well stow it. If you two bilge rats got nothing better to do I've got some decks that need swabbing."

"I've gotta get back on watch anyway. See you guys later," Nagle said shoving back from the table.

"The Boatswain's in a foul mood, huh?" Anderson commented after the chief had left the mess deck.

"Yeah, I guess he's got a lot on his..."

"Now set the sea and anchor detail!" the 21-mc suddenly screeched. "Now set the sea and anchor detail! All hands prepare to get underway."

****

"It's gotta be hard on those guys," Marty the bartender said to a waitress as they stood by a huge picture window watching the *USS Kamey* sail past the Mayport Acey-Ducy Club, "especially the married guys that have families living in the area."

"Yeah it's gotta suck," the waitress, a petite brunette who had joked around with the Kamey sailors the night before agreed. "They weren't expecting to leave again until sometime next year."

Chapter 5

Kamey had barely cleared the Mayport ship channel when the squawk box once again roared to life, "Now set Modified Condition ZEBRA! Set Modified Condition ZEBRA!"

Instantly sailors throughout the ship sprang into action closing all doors, scuttles, hatches port holes and fittings marked with a black X or Y. Modified condition zebra allowed movement throughout the ship yet maintained the ship's water-tight integrity.

"Well now," Chief Jeff Curtis exclaimed, entering the R Division Shipfitter Shop and spinning the handle on the watertight door behind him. "Maybe now we'll find out what's going on."

"Isn't it sort of unusual to set condition zebra this soon out?" asked an R Division sailor.

"That it is, me laddie, that it is," Petty Officer Anderson answered. "That's your first clue that is this more than just another drill."

Anderson, a Korean War veteran had served aboard the destroyer *USS Gurke,* one of five U.S. destroyers tasked with the bombardment of Wolmi-Do island leading up to General Douglas MacArthur's amphibious invasion of Inchon.

Despite three direct hits from Communist gunfire, *Gurke's* 5-inch batteries continued her shore bombardment while Anderson and his damage control party put out fires and repaired the damage.

"So whatta you think Chief, is this just another drill or what? Anderson asked.

"Don't know Andy. Goat locker rumor says we're heading for Cuba."

Fireman Apprentice Harvey Leonard, a chubby 18-year-old sailor from Batesville, Mississippi, wrinkled his brow and whispered to Anderson, "What's a goat locker"?

"Hey Chief," Anderson laughed, "This landlubber here, wants to know what a goat locker is."

"Goat locker is a slang term for Chief's Quarters," Chief Curtis said. "In early sailing days there was no refrigeration on board ships so a goat was brought aboard to supply the crew with fresh milk. Problem was; who would be responsible for caring for the goat. Even back then, chiefs were the most responsible individuals on board, so the goat was kept in the chiefs' quarters where it would be properly fed and taken care of. That me lad, according to Navy lore, is where the term Goat Locker comes from."

"Thanks, chief," Leonard said, grabbing onto an overhead pipe as the ship took a sudden heavy roll to starboard.

"Feels like we're in for some rough weather. Warden, grab a couple of guys and make sure everything's buttoned down topside," the chief instructed. "If you need me I will be in the Chief's Quarters.

On the bridge Captain Feeney came to the same conclusion as he watched heavy waves break over the bow. "Get me the latest weather report," he said to the quartermaster of the watch.

"The National Weather Service reports a tropical depression developing near the Bahamas," Quartermaster Second Class James Norton reported a few moments later.

"According to the latest forecast it could became a tropical storm within the next 10-12 hours."

"Our luck sure seems to be holding, doesn't it," the XO said. "What's next I wonder ... a full-fledged hurricane?

"I wouldn't be the least bit surprised Paul," the Captain responded. "Our luck sure seems to be running in that direction lately. Make sure the deck department is ready for heavy weather and keep all unnecessary personnel off the weather decks."

"Aye, aye Captain," the XO responded as he left the bridge.

Chapter 6

Some 200 miles northeast of the Bahamas the Soviet Foxtrot class submarine *B-132* under the command of Captain Second Rank Vladimir Sumkov was also encountering weather related problems. *B-132*, a diesel powered submarine, had to periodically surface to recharge its batteries. Under normal conditions Sumkov would use his snorkel, a device perfected by the Germans during World War II, to permit a submarine to expel exhaust and take in fresh air to run the diesels while submerged just below the surface. But the storm raging on the surface ruled out snorkeling. Turbulence created by the rough seas would make life aboard the submarine nearly unbearable.

Looking about the control room, studying the faces of his weary crew, the veteran submariner took a quick peek at the worsening sea state through the periscope as he mulled over his current dilemma. Surely navy leaders in Moscow must have known that at this time of year *B-132* would likely encounter tropical weather as it approached the shipping lanes along the American East Coast. That lack of forethought, Sumkov reasoned, could spell potential disaster for *B-132* and the other three Foxtrots of the four-boat Anadyr Group sailing under strict secrecy for their new home port at the Cuban Marier Naval Base on the northwestern coast of the island nation.

[42]

Sumkov was also keenly aware of the enormous responsibility he and other submarine commanders had regarding the possible use of the nuclear weapons each submarine carried. During a top secret briefing by the Commander of the Northern Fleet prior to sailing, he had asked the assembled flag officers about the rules of engagement for use of nuclear torpedoes if he, or the other submarine commanders, were confronted with unexpected or unusual situations. As he had expected, the replies were cryptic and foreboding.

"Once your face has been slapped Comrade Captain, don't let them slap your face again," one of the admirals had snapped. The other assembled senior officers nodded approvingly. This simple statement shifted the awesome responsibility for the possibility of starting World War III from the Kremlin, directly to the shoulders of Sumkov and his fellow submarine commanders. For most of the western world this would have been an unconscionable act of bureaucratic and personal cowardice, but for the Soviets it had been a common practice since the days of Joseph Stalin.

The four nuclear-armed submarines had departed their base on October 1, at thirty minute intervals. *B-132* was the last to leave.

Rounding the North Cape separating the stormy snow squalls of the Barents Sea from the Atlantic Ocean, Sumkov was painfully aware of the Cold War tension between the Soviet Union and the United States and was aware that this mission, and the top secret device resting in the forward torpedo room, could push the world over the brink.

As he watched the intricate operations by his well-trained crew, Sumkov realized that his superiors had selected him and his submarine for the Anadyr operation because he was one of the few Soviet submarine commanders who had actually fired a 10-kiloton torpedo. Because of his success with the torpedo naval leaders assumed that in the event of a war Sumkov would successfully fire the deadly fish, despite the realization that the havoc would almost certainly destroy *B-132* and its entire crew.

What Sumkov or his fellow submariners didn't know however, was that Soviet ICBM missile launch sites were already under construction in Cuba and that the young American President, John F. Kennedy, was determined to prevent them from ever becoming operational.

****

Atlantic Fleet Mobile Photographic Group
Naval Air Station, Norfolk, Va.

Commander Jack Sermons, Officer-in Charge of the Navy's highly elite Atlantic Fleet Mobile Photographic Group read the message he had received from Commander-in-Chief Atlantic, for the umpteenth time. "How in the hell am I supposed to do this?" he wondered out loud.

Laying the message on his desk he reached for his ever present coffee mug, grunted that it was empty and proceeded, first to the unit coffee mess to refill the mug with hot, strong black coffee, then directly to the Leading Chiefs office. "Mac, how many photo mates do we have on deployment?"

"Hmmm, let's see here," the veteran chief photographer said reaching for a file titled Deployment Log half hidden in the clutter on his desk. "As of this morning we have, aah…twenty-two men on deployment. That includes three motion picture teams with soundmen."

"Any of them in the Caribbean?"

"Yes sir. We have a mopic team and five still photographers assigned to Operation Ortsac; one still photographer at Rosy Roads and one at NAS Bermuda, in case that storm brewing in the Caribbean causes damage at either of those bases and of course, we have a permanent four man detachment at Gitmo."

"How many are air crew qualified?"

"About half. Why do you ask, Sir?"

"We're going to have to do some shuffling around chief," Sermons said. "We've just gotten some major new tasking from CINCLANT. Get all available crew chiefs together and meet me in the conference room in 30 minutes."

"Gents I don't have to tell you that the current geopolitical situation has spread us pretty thin," the Atlantic Fleet Mobile Photographic Group boss told the half-dozen assembled photo warrant and chief petty officers. And, starting right now, Mobile Photo is going to be spread even thinner. CINCLANT has ordered aerial and surface photo coverage of every facet of Operation Ortsac and a new classified operation called Blue Moon."

"That'll mean recalling most of the European detachments," Chief MacDonald said.

"So be it. I'm pretty sure CINCLANT considers this a little more important than a Navy feel good PR story. In the meantime, contact every photo mate we have on assignment in the Caribbean and direct them to standby for further orders. Fleet Air Photo at Jacksonville and Key West pretty much have aerial coverage under control. So our biggest concern is surface coverage.

"Let's try to assign a photographer's mate to as many small surface ships as possible. The carriers and larger combatants already have photo mates aboard but we'll have to get someone aboard the destroyers. Chief Smith," Sermons said to the admin chief, "get blanket orders cut for the admiral's signature, directing full co-operation of commanding officers in providing full and unrestricted access for photographers, regardless of rank."

****

USS Kamey

"Fleet tug out of NAS Bermuda requesting to come along side to disembark passengers Sir," the duty signalman reported to the OOD after reading a flashing light message from a short, stout looking vessel powering its way through turbulent seas.

"Maybe it's our missing crewmembers Captain," the OOD said to Captain Feeney.

"They picked a hell of a time to get them back to us didn't they? Feeney replied. "Bring them up on ship-to-ship."

"*Kamey* this is fleet tug *Mosopelea,* with ten souls aboard in transit *USS Kamey*." The voice on the other end of the ship-to-ship phone said. "Seven *Kamey* crewmembers, two pilots; en route *USS Randolph,* and one photographer's mate for temporary duty aboard *Kamey*."

"What the hell do I need a shutter clicker for?" Feeney mumbled under his breath.

"Very well *Mosopelea*, come alongside, and proceed with extreme caution."

"Standby to receive passengers from *USS Mosopelea*. Escort the photographer directly to the bridge," the Captain ordered.

****

"PH2 Ty Stephens reporting as ordered, Sir," the slender, red-headed photographer's mate said holding a firm salute.

"Stand at ease Petty Officer Stephens," Captain Feeney responded returning the salute. "Welcome aboard. I'm sort of confused as to why you're here though. I assume you have written orders?"

"Yes Sir," Stephens said retrieving a worn brownish envelope from the camera bag dangling from his shoulder and handing it to the skipper.

"You have been fully briefed on your assignment, I assume?" Feeney asked after reading the documents.

"I know that I am supposed to document all naval contact with foreign vessels and get the film back to Norfolk as quickly as possible, Sir."

"It also says you're to have unrestricted access to all parts of the ship. So I guess that means you'll need to be as close to the bridge and CIC as possible. Anything special you need?

"Not much, Sir, maybe a small dark area, with running water, where I can process film."

Mr. Jason get Petty Officer Stephens settled in my sea cabin. You should be able to use the head there to process your film."

"Yes Sir. This way Stephens, have any other gear?" the junior officer of the deck asked glancing at the photographer's camera bag.

"Just a small knapsack with an extra camera body, couple of lenses, couple bricks of film, a change of clothing and a few personal items."

"I'll see that it's stowed in the Captain's sea cabin. You'll take your meals in the crews mess. By the way I'm Lt.(jg) Larry Jason, assistant communications /public affairs officer and a devoted amateur photographer," he said extending his right hand to Stephens.

"When things settle down a little maybe we can get together and shoot the breeze about photography. In the meantime, if I can be of any assistance don't hesitate to let me know."

"Thank you, Sir." Stephens replied, sliding the camera bag off his shoulder and looking about the tiny room. "Hummm — I would have thought the commanding officer of a Navy warship would have more luxurious accommodations," the photographer grinned.

"Now you know why destroyers are called small boys or tin cans. We get bounced around a lot and don't have much in the way of creature comforts," Jason grinned. "The skipper's stateroom is only a slight improved over this, but still, they are slightly better accommodations than most of the crew has. Good talking with you Stephens, I better get back on the bridge before you see a different side of the Old Man," Jason chuckled as he departed the room.

After stowing his gear, Stephens checked to ensure that his camera was loaded and went out on the weather deck just as a huge blue-green wave broke over the bow.

The pitching of the ship intensified even more and suddenly there was a loud CLINK, CLAP, CLANK coming from the torpedo deck.

Grabbing the rails of the ladder leading down to the torpedo deck Stephens, glanced over the side and saw an acetylene bottle, which had broken loose from its storage rack sliding about the deck.

"Ah shit," Stephens cried out, quickly changing the settings on his camera to 1/200 of a second at f/8 and indiscriminately pressing the shutter button as he lowered himself slowly down the ladder. "If the top of that thing goes it's going to explode," he said aloud continuing on down the ladder.

****

"Yes sir. We'll take care of it." Chief Jeff Curtis said hanging up the phone in the Shipfitter Shop. "Anderson, Leonard, we've got an acetylene bottle loose on the main deck. Grab your foul weather gear and get up there and secure it before the damn thing knocks a hole in the bulkhead. Be careful out there guys, the bridge says the

[49]

weather has really turned nasty. Make sure you have safety lines on."

Forcing the amidships watertight door open against the howling wind, Petty Officer Anderson and Fireman Apprentice Leonard came face-to-face with the visiting shutterbug, hanging on to the torpedo deck ladder with one hand while trying to keep his Nikon dry with the other.

"Captain you've gotta see this," said the OOD, standing outside on the flying bridge pointing toward the main deck.

"Who the hell is that?"

"I'm guessing it's our visiting photographer, Stephens," replied the OOD.

"Well get his ass inside before he's washed overboard," Captain Feeney snapped.

"Yes sir. I don't guess we have to worry about him having his sea legs, do we?" the duty officer laughed.

After securing the floundering acetylene bottle, Anderson grabbed Stephens by the arm while Leonard grabbed his shirt and led the soaked photographer's mate to the amidships watertight door and pushed him inside.

"What the hell were you doing out there man?" Anderson yelled. "You trying to get your dumb ass killed?"

Wiping the seawater from his face, Stephens merely grinned and said, "That's where the pictures are man. No one ever got pictures worth a shit sitting on their ass inside a cozy compartment."

<u>Chapter 7</u>

Despite attempts by the White House and the Pentagon to maintain a low profile on developments in the Caribbean, rumors of a planned Cuban invasion persisted and a quick return from Seattle where the President was attending the opening of the World's Fair only added fuel to the fire. At a press briefing at the White House, the president's press secretary told the media that the President had flown back to Washington on the advice of his personal physician because he was suffering from an upper respiratory infection.

While the press secretary was doing his best to convince a skeptical press corps, the President and his advisers were pouring over the latest reconnaissance photographs, including several close-up views, taken by a Cuban-based CIA photographer, of an ICBM being off loaded from a Soviet ship at the port of Bahia del Mariel, and concluded that the United States had three choices: negotiate with the Soviets to try and get them to remove the missiles; bomb the missile sites; or implement a naval blockade of the island.

The President favored the blockade idea because it allowed the Soviets an opportunity to back off without losing face. A politically astute State Department official, however, suggested that the word quarantine be substituted for blockade.

"Blockade," the official reminded the President, "is defined under international treaties as an act of war. Quarantine, on the other hand merely implies that unwanted materials are to be kept out of a particular area. With the mere change of a word, we can completely choke off the island of Cuba without the international community considering it an act of war."

"Quarantine it is then. Good catch," the President smiled.

All ships bound for Cuba, regardless of registry were to be stopped... by force if necessary. The Pentagon chiefs, however, insisted that an air attack option should the blockade... i.e. quarantine fail, be kept open.

****

Soviet Submarine B-132

Sumkov's first encounter with the American Navy came within hours of the President's decision. *B-132* sailors were monitoring commercial radio programs for information and entertainment while running at periscope depth off the coast of Key West when all commercial radio frequencies, normally available to ships at sea, suddenly became uncharacteristically quiet.

At about the same time a *B-132* radioman monitoring naval radio frequencies from Roosevelt Roads and Bermuda picked up a transmission from a ground station to a Navy

[52]

P-2V Neptune antisubmarine aircraft giving the exact position of *B-132*.

"Are you quiet sure you understood the transmission correctly comrade," Sumkov questioned the radio operator who reported the transmission.

"Aye, Comrade Captain, the radioman replied.

Moments later the approaching aircraft was detected by radar and confirmed by a visual sighting.

"Dive!" Sumkov ordered. "Take her down to 300 feet with a 90-degree change in course to port."

Once under the seas, *B-132's* skipper realized that he could soon be facing American surface forces and, given the condition of his submarine, he was worried that it would be difficult if not impossible to evade them. In complying with standard operations, he ordered the radio operator to report the Neptune contact. Without any knowledge of the larger events taking place on the surface, Captain Second Rank Vladimir Sumkov had sailed *B-132* and its nuclear torpedo across the proposed American quarantine line.

****

USS Kamey
October 22, 1962

"Urgent message, from CINCLANT Captain," the communications officer said, bursting through the bridge door.

Captain Feeney quickly read the brief message, shook his head in disbelief and read it again, this time scanning every word with extreme care.

"Looks like all hell is about to break lose Paul," he said to the executive officer who had just arrived on the bridge. Staring at the green waves breaking over the bow, his voice barely audible, he said, "Let's go to general quarters."

BONG! BONG! BONG! "General Quarters, General Quarters. All hands man your battle stations. This is not a drill. This is not a drill. Set ASW Condition One. All hands man your battle stations."

Without a designated GQ station *Kamey's* visiting photographer grabbed his two Nikon F cameras, one fitted with a 24mm lens the other with a 200mm; and headed for the bridge, just forward of the Captain's sea cabin. "OK if I stay on the bridge and take a few photos, sir?" Stephens asked the XO.

"Yea, fine," the executive officer growled, "just don't get in the way."

When the last of the "manned and ready reports" were received on the bridge, the Captain addressed the crew.

"This is the Captain speaking. Over the past few days all of us have been on edge and very much in the dark about what is going on. After nearly seven and half months in the Med we were looking forward to a well deserved rest and time with our families and then we were abruptly ordered back to sea.

"A few moments ago *Kamey* received an urgent message from CINCLANT which may finally shine some light on what the secrecy is all about. At 2000 this evening, President John F. Kennedy will address the nation, regarding the possible deployment of Soviet nuclear missiles on the island of Cuba. The President's address will be patched throughout the ship. All hands are strongly encouraged to listen. That is all."

"Paul," Captain Feeney said to the XO, as he replaced the 21-MC handset back in its bulkhead mounded cradle, "have all officers and chiefs assemble in the Wardroom immediately after the president's address. Oh, and bring the shutter clicker along," he said nodding his head in the direction of Petty Officer Stephens as he snapped pictures of the hodgepodge of expressions being displayed by bridge personnel, as each man in his own way, tried to comprehend what was happening.

As though on cue, the moment the squawk box went silent chiefs and leading petty officers in every department and division aboard *Kamey* spring into action. Despite the fact — that as a result of its hasty departure —

Kamey was vastly undermanned, *Kamey's* senior enlisted men, many of whom were veterans of World War II and the Korean War, were determined to do whatever was necessary to ensure that their rugged little warship was ready to meet any and all challenges.

****

"What's up Gunner?" Stephens asked Chief Gunner's Mate Leon Allen as the chief exited the forward number two 5-inch gun mount. "Think you'll be firing those things anytime soon?"

"Can't say, but we'll damned well be ready if we have too. Make damn sure that ready locker is full and ready to go," he barked at a frightened looking gunner's mate striker. "I sure as hell don't want to run out of ammo if anything does happen.

"Get Donaldson or one of those other slackers who just came aboard up here to help you," he snapped. "Oh, and make sure the watch is relieved in time for chow. We might be in for a long evening," Allen said as he proceed aft to check on the after gun mounts.

****

Sipping a cup of black coffee on the crowded mess deck, which also served as a battle dressing station during general quarters, Stephens along with dozen other off-duty *Kamey* crewmembers listened intently as the unmistakable Bostonian accent of the President of the United States boomed from speakers throughout the hardy little warship.

"Good evening my fellow citizens"

"Within the past week, we have received unmistakable evidence of a massive Soviet military buildup on the Island of Cuba which includes a series of offensive missile sites. The purpose of these bases can be none other than to provide a nuclear strike capability against the Western Hemisphere.

Acting, therefore, in the defense of our own security and of the entire Western Hemisphere, and under the authority entrusted to me by the Constitution as endorsed by the resolution of the Congress, I have directed that the following initial steps be taken immediately.

First: To halt this offensive buildup, a strict quarantine on all offensive military equipment under shipment to Cuba is being initiated. All ships of any kind bound for Cuba from whatever nation or port will, if found to contain cargoes of offensive weapons, be turned back. This quarantine will be extended, if needed, to other types of cargo and carriers.

Second: I have directed the continued and increased close surveillance of Cuba and its military buildup. Should these offensive military preparations continue, thus increasing the threat to this hemisphere, further action will be justified. I have directed the Armed Forces to prepare for any eventualities.

Third: It shall be the policy of this nation to regard any nuclear missile launched from Cuba against any nation in the Western Hemisphere as an attack by the Soviet Union on the United States, requiring a full retaliatory response upon the Soviet Union.

Fourth: As a necessary military precaution, I have reinforced our base at Guantanamo, evacuated today the dependents of our personnel there, and ordered additional military units to be placed on a standby alert.

My fellow citizens: let no one doubt that this is a difficult and dangerous effort on which we have set out. No one can see precisely what course it will take or what costs or casualties will be incurred. Many months of sacrifice and self-discipline lie ahead — months in which our patience will be tested — months in which many threats and denunciations will keep us aware of our dangers. But the greatest danger of all would be to do nothing.

The path we have chosen for the present is full of hazards, as all paths are — but it is the one most consistent with our character and courage as a nation and our commitments around the world. The cost of freedom is always high — and Americans have always paid it. And one path we shall never choose is the path of surrender or submission.

Our goal is not the victory of might, but the vindication of right — not peace at the expense of freedom, but both peace and freedom here in this hemisphere and, we hope, around the world. God willing, that goal will be achieved.

Thank you and good night.

****

Although the Soviets had received an advance copy of the president's speech, Castro and the Cuban government learned of it at the same time as the American people. In response to the speech Castro immediately mobilized

Cuba's military forces to protect the Island Nation in the event of an American invasion.

Castro had feared an American invasion since coming to power three years earlier and was plainly aware of several thinly veiled U.S. attempts to oust him, starting with the Bay of Pigs fiasco eighteen months earlier and most recently a major U.S. military exercise in the Caribbean named Operation Ortsac. Castro was convinced that Operation Ortsac was nothing more than a planning operation for a U.S. invasion of Cuba.

Chapter 8

The earlier jovial mood of *Kamey* crewmembers suddenly turned to one of somber disbelief as the destroyermen
struggled to comprehend what they had just heard. As
confusion, fear, anger and skepticism registered on the
faces of the crew, Stephens readjusted the settings of his
camera and rested it on top of an ice machine to com-
pensate for the three-second exposures he was forced to
use in trying to capture the agony and bewilderment fro-
zen on the faces of the sailors assembled on the crowded,
smoke-filled, crew's mess deck. The chatter was
drowned out by the sudden squeal of the 1-mc.

"All officers and chief petty officers please report to the
Wardroom."

****

"Gentlemen!" the Captain said without the customary in-
troductory remarks, "We're one step away from a nuclear war. Our job is two-fold: prevent all seaborne traffic
from entering or leaving Cuban ports without first being
searched, and second, seek out and bring to the surface,
any Soviet submarine that may be operating in the area.
As of this moment we are a part of Hunter-Killer Group
Bravo. Any ship bound for Cuba will be stopped and

boarded, by force if necessary, and searched for war-making cargo."

"And if the ship doesn't stop?" Lt. Commander Bolton queried.

"In accordance with our orders, we'll fire across the ship's bow, and if it still fails to stop, we'll blow off the rudder to stop forward progress. Any foreign submarines detected in the quarantine area will be requested, via so-nobuoy, to surface and be identified."

"Then what?" the XO asked.

"They will be directed to reverse course and leave the quarantine area."

"If the sub commander decides not to surface, do we attack?" the weapons officer asked.

"Let's hope it doesn't come to that. But, in the event a sub doesn't comply, we are to drop three hand grenades in the water — at one minute intervals — to let them know we're serious. After the third grenade, then yes, the sub will be subject to attack. The Soviets, according to CINCLANT, have been notified of the submarine identifying procedure and we fully expect they will comply."

After a few more questions, the Captain ended the all officers and chiefs meeting by reminding them that *Kamey*, indeed the entire fleet, was now operating under strict wartime conditions.

"We'll remain at a modified GQ," Feeney said, "but please stress to your troops that all normal ship's work must continue. Based on the information I've received from the task group commander the best Intel we have is that the closest surface vessel to the quarantine line is a Soviet tanker which, if it maintains its current speed and course, is expected to cross the line at approximately 0930 tomorrow morning"

"What about Soviet warships, other than submarines Captain," the XO asked, "are they to be handled the same as merchant ships?"

"There are no known foreign warships, with the possible exception of a submarine or two, operating in these waters and submarines don't announce their presence. But, in the unlikely event we should encounter a Soviet surface warship, it too would be challenged. Questions?"

"Yes sir. How do we respond if a Soviet cargo ship or warship fires upon us," the weapons officer asked.

"We sink his dumb ass." Lt. Commander. Bolton replied.

"Anything more to add, XO?" the Captain asked fighting to hold back a snicker in response to Bolton's comment.

"Stress to your troops that we are sailing into uncharted waters and everyone should stay on their toes. Urge them to try and get a good night's sleep. Tomorrow is shaping up to be an exciting day. We will be going alongside the carrier *Lexington* to top off our fuel tanks tomorrow morning and will remain with *Lexington* for the rest of the day to provide plane guard duty."

****

"So, whatta you think Andy? Petty Officer Warden asked Frank Anderson, "Think this will be anything like Korea."

"Who knows what the politicians have up their sleeve," Anderson replied as he removed his towel and shaving kit from his locker in preparation to go the showers. "The only thing you can count on is the fact that it will be the lower echelon military, as usual, carrying the load if war does come about."

"Yeah, maybe so, but don't you think Kennedy, being a famous Navy war hero, understands what the peons have to go through when the shooting starts?"

"You would think so, wouldn't you? See you later Warden, I want to get to the showers before all the fresh water is gone."

"Hey, why don't you see if you can get that shutter-clicker to take a picture of you so you can send it to your wife," Warden laughed as the damage controlman exited the berthing compartment.

"No need," Anderson yelled over his shoulder, "she is fully aware of what she's missing."

Chapter 9

October 23, 1962—0500

"REVEILLE! REVEILLE!" All hands on deck; trice up all bunks. Commence clean sweep down fore and aft. REVEILLE! REVEILLE!"

"Ahhh shit!" Photographer's Mate Stephens moaned, rubbing his eyes. Following the president's speech the night before, Stephens had roamed throughout the ship until the wee hours of the morning, snapping photos of enlisted and officer crew members as they discussed the possible ruminations of current events and how they might affect their life and careers.

"Damn," protested a boiler technician who had been due to retire after 23 years in the Navy. "I have a job lined up with Ingalls Shipyard in Pascagoula. I have an interview scheduled for November 12 and if everything goes well I'm supposed to report for work January 7. Damn!"

"Don't sweat it," the chief boiler tech told him, "if the Russkies or Cubans launch a nuclear missile you want need a job anyway. There won't be anything left to go home too."

After filling up several notebook pages with those sorts of doom's day comments and exposing several rolls of film, Stephens, at around 0300, had decided to call it a night. Springing from the bunk, Stephens went into the Captain's small sea cabin bathroom, splashed water on his face, brushed his teeth and went to the crews mess for breakfast.

Descending the starboard outside ladder to the main deck, en route to the mess deck, he couldn't help but notice the vast difference in the sea state. Huge angry waves of the night before had given way to a slight chop. The golden sun rising over the eastern horizon revealed that *Kamey* now shared the clear emerald-blue Caribbean waters with a host of other warships including the carrier *USS Lexington* steaming a mile or so off *Kamey's* starboard bow.

As Stephens approached the hatch leading to the mess decks he encountered Lt. (jg) Larry Jason heading for the wardroom.

"Looks like it's going to be a great day for taking pictures," the assistant communications officer said.

"Sure is. By the way sir, would it create a problem if I shot pictures from up there," Stephens asked pointing to a small platform near the top of main mast.

"I don't know 'bout that. That's a pretty dangerous place to be taking pictures from. I'll have to check with the XO."

"Thank you sir," Stephens said taking his place in the chow line. The roving photographer had just sat down with a tray of scrambled eggs, sausage and grits when the mess deck chatter was suddenly curtailed by the warbling of the boatswain's pipe.

"Now set the refueling detail. The smoking lamp is out

throughout the ship."

"There you go picture man," a sailor seated across the table from Stephens said. "Underway replenishment always makes for good pictures. I'll show you some of the best places to shoot from if you would like."

"Well, ah, thank, you...huh..."

"Wilson. Joe Wilson, I'm a boatswain's mate striker," the sailor said smiling.

"Thanks, I appreciate it. You into photography Joe?"

"Yeah, I shot tons of photos on our last deployment. Mr. Jason said he would like to use some of them in the cruise book."

"That's great man. I would like to see some of your pictures. Ever thought about maybe getting into Navy photography?"

"Actually I have, but I'm a black shoe and photography is an Airedale rate."

"That's actually a myth," Stephens corrected. "Yes photography is assigned to the aviation ratings branch. But photographers are Airedales in name only.

Photographers can be assigned to anything. At sea we serve aboard carriers, cruisers, submarines, tenders, you name it. Photo mates also serve with the Seabees and Marines. Any place where there might be a need for photo documentation you will find a Navy or Marine Corps photographer. Check into it. You might just find yourself in Pensacola going through photo school before you know it."

Climbing the ladder to the torpedo deck with his new found friend, Stephens, although he had seen aircraft carriers before from aircraft and ashore, was amazed at the size of the veteran World War II aircraft carrier, in comparison to the destroyer, as *Kamey* slowly approached *USS Lexington* from the starboard quarter.

****

While *Kamey* was topping off her fuel tanks, some 200 miles away the aircraft carrier *USS Lake Champlain,* accompanied by the destroyer *USS Joseph P. Kennedy* were making contact with the Soviet tanker *Bucharest* which had just passed the outer quarantine line.

While helicopters from *Lake Champlain* circled overhead, *Kennedy* ordered the ship, via flashing light, to stand by for boarding and inspection of her cargo. After a delay of nearly an hour the bureaucrats in Washington decided that the *Bucharest* carried no contraband cargo and was allowed to continue her voyage on to Havana without being searched.

Word of the *Kennedy* encounter with the Soviet tanker quickly spread throughout the hunter-killer group.

"Hell if all we are going to do is shake hands with the Russkies why are we sweating our ass off at general quarters," Lt. Commander Bolton, aboard *USS Kamey* asked rhetorically. "What are we going to do the next time we encounter a ship running the blockade, invite the crew aboard for tea?"

"Take it easy Paul," the Captain ordered, "we're not involved with the political crap. We just carry out our orders."

****

[67]

Washington D.C.
The White House

In the nation's capital tensions continued to build, as President Kennedy read the latest message from Soviet Premier Nikita Khrushchev:

> *"Mr. President, you are not declaring quarantine but threatening that if we do not give in to your demands you will use force. No Mr. President I cannot agree to this, and I think that in your own heart you recognize that I am correct. I am convinced that in my place you would act the same way.*
>
> *Therefore, Mr. President, the Soviet Government cannot instruct the Captains of Soviet vessels bound for Cuba to observe the orders of the American naval forces blockading that Island.... If you insist on these piratical acts by American ships on the high seas, we will be forced to take whatever measures we consider necessary and adequate to protect our rights."*

"How should we reply, Mr. President?" the National Security Advisor asked.

"National security must come first, George. We can't negotiate with a gun at our head. If they won't remove the missiles and restore the status quo, we will have to do it ourselves."

"I fully agree, Mr. President," said Defense Secretary McNamara. "The Soviets have placed offensive weapons a mere 90 miles from our shores and that can't be tolerated."

Soviet Submarine B-132

Captain Second Rank Vladimir Sumkov slowly maneuvered *B-132* upward to snorkeling depth. A quick peek through the periscope revealed that the seas were now fairly calm and he should be able to charge *B-132's* batteries and perhaps allow the crew to go on deck, a few at a time, to get some desperately needed fresh air.

"Prepare to charge batteries," Sumkov ordered.

"We only have one workable engine Comrade Captain," the chief engineer reported. "The storm wrecked two of the diesels and we can't repair them at sea."

"Are you telling me we can't charge the batteries with the one working engine we do have?"

"We can charge them, Comrade Captain, but the charge will only last for an hour or two and it will have to be charged again."

"Very well, do the best you can and keep the engineers working on the damaged engines."

"Comrade Captain," *B-132's* radar operator shouted. We've detected an American aircraft carrier and its escort ships directly ahead."

"How far away?"

"Maybe ten miles dead ahead."

With his submarine nearly without power, Sumkov knew he had to keep charging for as long as possible. If he could remain undetected for an hour at the most maybe he could dive and evade the power of the American

Navy ... maybe.

"Keep me informed of the American ships' course and speed, comrade," Sumkov said to the sonar operator. "We must continue charging for as long as possible. We will proceed at snorkel depth until we have visual contact with the Americans," Sumkov told his second in command. "Standby to dive when I give the order."

****

USS Kamey

Captain Feeney, reclining in the Captain's chair on the bridge, sipping a cup of coffee, was momentary started when an excited voice boomed from the squawk box.

"Bridge-Sonar: Contact bearing zero five zero!"

"Sonar-Bridge: Contact classification?" Feeney replied, raising his binoculars to his eyes.

"Bridge-Sonar: Can't say for certain Captain, but it appears to be a Foxtrot class."

"Stay with him sonar and let me know his every move."

"Bridge-Sonar: Aye, aye, Sir, I'm on his tail."

Captain Feeney had no doubt about maintaining contact. There was no better sonar man in the entire Navy than SO1 Jack Reed. According to his fellow sonar techs, Reed could hear a barracuda taking a crap at 3,000 feet.

"I've got the Conn," Feeney said calmly, to the OOD. "Right full rudder, make turns for fifteen knots. Set anti-submarine condition one."

Hearing the order for ASW condition one, Stephens hastened towards the bow. Scanning the horizon through a 300mm lens and seeing nothing, he went to the bridge.

"You might want to hang close," Captain Feeney said when Stephens entered from the portside open bridge. "We've got ourselves what appears to be a Soviet sub. If he surfaces, and he will, I want pictures. Oh, and Stephens, I don't want to see any more asinine stunts like you pulled with the acetylene bottle, understood."

"Aye, aye, Sir."

****

Soviet Submarine B-132

Having decided to continue running near the surface to charge his near depleted batteries, Sumkov grew tense about making visual contact with the approaching ASW group. His thoughts instantly turned to the nuclear torpedo resting in one of his forward torpedo tubes. Depending on what the Americans did, he could be forced to fire the torpedo and then dive and hope that his ship-handling skills would pull them through this precarious situation. Doing so, Sumkov realized, would surely lead to nuclear hostilities between the Soviet Union and the United States, killing millions of people in both nations.

Faced with this terrible alterative Sumkov changed his mind and ordered his executive officer to dive the boat, shutting down the noisy diesel engine. Within moments of slipping completely beneath the waves, the diving officer reported that the sub's dive planes wouldn't fully deploy. Instead of providing a measure of security and the promise of possibly evading the approaching Americans, technical problems continued to haunt the veteran submariner.

While Sumkov and his key officers were considering ways to escape the American warships, the lead sonar man reported a series of explosions a few feet above and on the port side of *B-132's* position. The American destroyer *USS Kamey* was sixty feet overhead waiting for the Soviet commander's next move.

"Take the boat to 400 feet and rig for silent running," Sumkov ordered.

As the submarine passed the 350-foot mark a propulsion cooling line which drew water from the sea developed a major leak, allowing seawater to flood the engine room. As the alarm sounded throughout the boat, emergency crews string into action and quickly brought the flooding under control. With the ship nearly disabled and battery power getting lower by the minute, the executive officer urged Sumkov to surface.

"I'm sure the Americans will allow us to make repairs and be on our way, comrade Captain. What choice do they have? We haven't threatened them in any way and we are in international waters as are they."

Due to the strict radio silence policies Moscow demanded of its submarine crews, neither man knew of the tense situation which had developed between the Soviet Union and the United States over the past few days. Still, Captain Sumkov was reluctant. With an

American ASW group just a few hundred feet above, the risk of colliding with one of the American warships as the sub rose to the surface was just too great. Still, the flooding and steam filled propulsion spaces were becoming nearly uninhabitable.

"I suppose you are right comrade. Prepare to surface."

Before the order to surface could be issued, the chief engineer announced that flooding was under control and temporary repairs made by damage control personnel were holding. Thinking that perhaps his luck was finally turning for the better, Sumkov decided to remain submerged and try to maneuver out from under the task force and return to snorkeling depth.

In a desperate attempt to evade the Americans, Sumkov maneuvered his ship through a series of wide circles toward the surface, hoping to use the warm water near the surface to confuse *Kamey's* sonar. Within a matter of minutes the veteran undersea sailor realized that his plan was working.

****

USS Kamey

"Bridge-Sonar: We've lost him sir.

"Sonar-Bridge: Keep searching.

"Com-Bridge: Contact *Lexington* and request launch of ASW helos.

"Come to course three-two-zero, maintain 15 knots," he instructed the helmsman.

"We're dealing with one smart sub commander, Paul. This could turn into a real chess match before this day's over."

"We'll find him again skipper," the XO said smiling. "We've got the best sonar gang in the fleet. They didn't win the ASW Excellence Award three years in a row for sucking their thumbs. We'll get him back."

"I have no doubts about that, XO. If he's down there we'll find him ... and we know he's down there."

****

Soviet Submarine B-132

Sumkov's plan had worked. The constant rhythmic pinging of *Kamey's* active sonar against *B-132's* hull had stopped. But rather than head for the deep water of the Atlantic, as Captain Feeney had assumed, the submarine savvy Sumkov set a course for Cuba's Mariel naval base, his original destination.

****

The Pentagon War Room

"Admiral, the destroyer *Kamey* is dogging a Soviet sub and appears to be on the verge of forcing it to the surface. Grenades have been dropped in the water. Last report from *Kamey* said they had temporally lost sonar contact but expect to regain it at any moment."

"Tell the *Kamey's* skipper to maintain contact and stand by until the *USS Kennedy* arrives on the scene," the Secretary of Defense, standing within ear shot, said.

"Why are you doing that Sir?" The Chief of Naval Operations asked. "The *Kennedy* is more than a hundred miles away."

"The *Kennedy,* as you know, admiral, is named for the President's brother, Joseph, who was killed in World War II, and Bobby thinks it would be a good idea to let the *Joseph P. Kennedy* have the honor of being the first American ship to force a Soviet submarine to the surface. It will be great PR and good for crew morale."

"You've got to be kidding!" the Chief of Naval Operations roared. "God Damn it, Mr. Secretary, Bobby Kennedy has no say in what the Navy does; he is the Attorney General for crying aloud."

"He is also the President's younger brother. Now please relay my order to the *Kamey's* Captain"

"Aye, aye Mr. Secretary," the CNO said sarcastically. "But with all due respect, in the future, please remember that I'm in charge of naval operations ... not the Attorney General or you, Mr. Secretary."

****

Soviet Submarine B-132

With only one engine and dangerously low on battery power, Sumkov knew that *B-132* couldn't evade American surveillance for more than a few hours. *B-132's* sonar operator could hear the destroyers pinging and the search beginning anew.

Having been at sea for nearly twenty-six days, *B-132* had come to within 300 miles of Mariel but the veteran sub skipper knew that with the Americans drawing closer with each passing moment and *B-132's* problems increasing by the second, it would be impossible to reach Cuba without being forced to surface.

****

USS Kamey

It had been nearly an hour since *Kamey's* last contact and the ASW task group commander directed *Kamey* and the rest of the hunter-killer group to return to the point at which *B-132* had evaporated from their sonar and began a systematic search, and if contact was reestablished, to stand by until the *USS Joseph P. Kennedy, Jr.*, arrived on the scene.

Within minutes of lowering its towed-array variable-depth sonar transducer from the stern, the PING! PING! PING! of a positive contact reverberated throughout the lower decks of the destroyer. The cat and mouse game between *B-132* and *Kamey* had resumed and the cat was closing in.

"Captain, you're not going to believe this," Lieutenant (jg) Mark Waters, the communications officer, screamed waving a sheet of paper over this head, "you're just not going to believe it!"

Thrusting the message into the Captain's hands, Waters leaned against the bulkhead, wiped his brow and said, "Can you believe that crap Captain?"

"Has CINCLANTFLT lost his frigging mind," Captain Feeney said trying to comprehend what he was reading.

From: Commander Hunter-Killer Group Bravo
To: Commander USS Lexington ASW Force

Subj: USS Kamey submarine contact

*(1)   Kamey will maintain contact with unidentified sub-
marine but will take no action until USS Joseph P.
Kennedy, Jr. arrives on scene.*

*(2) Upon arrival of USS Kennedy, USS Kamey will assist
as necessary, in forcing submarine to surface.*

Captain Feeney started to hand the message to Lt. Commander Bolton, then quickly jerked if back and read it
again.

"Patch me through to the DesRon Sixteen flagship via
radiotelephone," he told the communications officer.

"Commodore Littlejohn, DesRon Sixteen, is on the on
the horn sir," Mark Waters said a few minutes later.

"Commodore; Captain Feeney here. CAN YOU TELL
ME, SIR, WHAT THE HELL IS GOING ON?" Feeney
screamed into the phone, totally ignoring all military
protocol. "*Kamey* has spent the last eighteen hours tracking this commie bastard and now we're supposed to let
the *Kennedy* take credit for bringing it to the surface?"

"Take it easy Captain," the Destroyer Squadron Sixteen
commander, said softly. "I know how you feel but it's a
direct order from the Secretary of Defense. It's a matter
of family pride for the Kennedy family. But I assure you
that the powers to be in Washington will know exactly
which ship was reasonable for the initial contact and the
surfacing."

"All due respect Commodore, but I'm sure that will
make my crew as happy as a pig in shit. They spent the
last seven months, away from home, busting their balls

in the Mediterranean while the *Kennedy* rested dockside, and now it's going to grab any glory there might be in surfacing this contact because the president's family thinks it's their birthright! I'm sorry, Sir, but we can't accept that," he snapped turning off the radiotelephone.

The sober tension was suddenly broken by an alert from sonar.

"Bridge-Sonar: Contact is behaving very erratically. It seems to going around in circles and we're picking up strange noises."

"Sonar-Bridge: What kind of noise. Could it be having some sort of mechanical problems?"

"Bridge-Sonar: Captain, this is Petty Officer Reed, a mechanical problem would be my guess sir. I have picked up what appears to be a hissing sound, like water striking a hot surface."

****

Soviet Submarine B-132

Sumkov's plan to try and confuse his nemesis above had worked for a while but now the conditions inside the submarine were getting worse by the minute and the only way he could make life better for the crew was to run on the surface and recharge his flawed batteries. Captain Second Rank Vladimir Sumkov decided that for the sake of his ship and its crew, it was time for the relentless submerged chase to end and gave the order to surface.

****

USS Kamey

"Bridge-Sonar: She's blowing ballast, sir. She's surfacing."

"We got the commie bastard," Feeney screamed slamming his fist down on the arm of the Captain's chair. "Screw those glory-grabbing assholes on the *Kennedy*, this joker is ours.

"Have the boarding party standby," he said to the officer of the deck, "just in case."

****

Soviet Submarine B-132

Slowly raising to periscope depth Sumkov rotated the periscope 90 degrees and was astonished to see the *USS Kamey* not more than sixty feet away. A mile or so to the left of his position the aircraft carrier *Lexington* was launching its H-3 anti-submarine helicopters. Two additional destroyers lurked just beyond *Lexington's* stern, definitely not a good position for a submarine to be in.

Broaching the surface, the first thing the veteran submariner noticed was a swarm of *Kamey* sailors, including one, with what appeared to be a telescope, perched on a small work platform high atop the *Kamey's* main-mast, pointing and taking pictures, as was a helicopter, now circling overhead. He realized of course that if the situation was reversed he would be doing the exact same thing. Gathering intelligence in these circumstances was only natural. His first priority, at the moment however, was to report *B-132's* predicament to Moscow.

"Send this immediately," he ordered the radio operator."

"Forced to surface after pursuit, battery low, drinking water nearly gone, two of three diesels disabled, surrounded by four American warships, awaiting instructions."

While waiting for a reply Sumkov pondered his next move. The Soviet Union and the United States, as far as he knew, were not at war. The biggest danger at the moment, Sumkov worried, was being rammed by an overzealous commander, sending *B-132* and its crew to the bottom in a politically motivated "accident." If however, the Americans did open fire on his submarine, then he could assume that the cold war had turned hot and respond accordingly.

In the meantime all he could do was to wait for guidance from his superiors in the Kremlin. The fact that *B-132* possessed a weapon that could easily destroy the entire hunter-killer task group offered little comfort. Sumkov was painfully aware that if he launched the 10-kiloton torpedo, *B-132* and its crew would perish as well. Even so, he was certain the crew would do their duty and follow orders.

After nearly an hour the naval command in Moscow finally responded, merely acknowledging receipt of his message and ordering *B-132* to return to base as best as he could, without offering any solutions to his current predicament.

****

USS Kamey

"Comm-Bridge: Contact Commander Hunter-Killer Group Bravo/DesRon Sixteen: Russian submarine on surface. Could not... repeat, could not, await arrival of *USS Joseph P. Kennedy*. Sub signaled it had an emergency and had to surface. *Kamey* standing by to lend assistance as needed."

"Stay alert people," Captain Feeney said to the bridge watch standers, as the shiny glistening conning tower broke the surface. "I don't think the sub commander would be foolish enough to try anything at this range, but we can't take any chances."

"Weapons-Bridge: We're going to lay off about 500 yards. Keep the forward five-inch mounts trained on both the hull and tower. If you see anyone pointing as much as a finger in our direction, open fire."

"Signal light from submarine, sir," the OOD said excitedly.

"What's he saying flags?" the skipper asked, using the common naval term for signalmen.

"Captain Sumkov commander Soviet submarine *B-132* sends greetings to the commander of the American destroyer."

"Ask if he needs assistance?"

The signalman's fingers became a blur as the young signalman flashed out a series of dots and dashes, relaying Feeney's message to the submarine commander.

"They are requesting drinking water sir," Signalman Second Class Chuck Shepherd answered moments later.

"Very well, tell them to come alongside. First Division rig potable water lines forward."

Comm-Bridge: Advise *Lexington* and DesRon Sixteen that submarine is coming alongside to receive drinking water.

"Get that shutter clicker down off the mast and send him to the focsule," the XO ordered the Boatswain's Mate of the Watch. "I want pictures of every damned Ruisskie who pops his head up on that sewer pipe."

"Holy shit!" Stephens exclaimed as he brought the face of Captain Second Rank Vladimir Sumkov, commander of the Russian submarine *B-132*, into sharp focus. "A real live Russian naval officer. Hell he looks just like us," Stephens said to BM2 Donald Patton, standing nearby.

"What the hell did you expect him to look like, shit for brains, some sort of horned fire breathing monster?"

"Ahhh, I guess that was a pretty stupid remark wasn't it?" the Navy photographer snickered.

"You think!" Patton said grabbing a heaving line tossed by a Russian sailor aboard *B-132*.

****

The White House
Oval Office

"Mr. President, the destroyer *USS Kamey* has gone to the aid of a Soviet submarine and the sub is now alongside *Kamey*," the Chief of Naval Operations told the President.

"Did *Kamey* attack the submarine? I gave explicit orders that submarines were to be identified only."

"No Sir, Mr. President, it wasn't attacked. The sub was apparently having some mechanical difficulties and the Captain made the decision to surface and asked *Kamey* for assistance.

"What sort of assistance," the president's brother asked.

"At this point Sir, we're not totally sure. It seems that the only thing the Russians have requested is fresh drinking water, which *Kamey* has provided."

"Thank you admiral," the President said, turning, his hands clasped behind his back, and looking out a window from behind his desk in the Oval Office.

After the CNO departed the President turned back to his brother, the Attorney General and asked, "Where's Bob?"

"I believe he is at the Pentagon sir."

"Get him on the line."

"Yes sir, Mr. President we have the situation under control," the Secretary of Defense told the Commander-in-Chief. The submarine is the *B-132,* an older diesel powered Foxtrot class.

Two of its three engines have been disabled and the commander had to surface before repairs could be attempted. The destroyer *Kamey* provided the sub with drinking water and *Lexington* lowered some fruit and other food items to them. They have declined offers of assistance with repairs.

"The submarine is now running on the surface, on an easterly course towards the Azores where a Soviet Navy tender is standing by. We'll keep the sub under surveillance in case it needs additional help until it meets up with the tender."

The *Lexington* ASW task group tailed *B-132* for the next several days as the submarine limped out into the open Atlantic. *Kamey* and another American destroyer took up a position 300 yards on either side and escorted the crippled submarine until it met up with the Soviet Navy tender.

****

After nearly a week on board the *Kamey*, Photographer's Mate Second Class Ty Stephens had nearly exhausted his film supply and during processing of the film in the make-shift darkroom he had set up in the Captain's sea cabin, he realized that many of his images probably had some intelligence value, but there was no doubt that they

[84]

all had the makings of several good photo essays. But regardless of how good his pictures were and how they might eventually be used, he first had to get them off the ship and back to the Mobile Photographic Group at Norfolk. The solution to his dilemma was steaming just a couple of miles ahead.

Hanging his latest roll of Tri-X up to dry, Stephens went to the bridge where he found Captain Feeney in his customary spot, relaxing in the Captain's chair, keeping a sharp eye on the carrier and the other ships making up the ASW task group.

"Excuse me Captain," Stephens said respectfully, "Could I speak with you, Sir."

"Of course Petty Officer Stephens, what can I do for you?"

"Well Sir, I've used up all but one roll of the film I brought aboard, and I need to get the pictures I have taken, back to Mobile Photo at Norfolk. So I was wondering, Sir, if you could get me aboard the *Lexington* where I might be able to grab a hop to Key West or Jacksonville."

"Well, now! I guess that's why they call you guys 'mobile photo,' huh, you're never in one place very long. Yeah, I think that can be arranged. We should be getting rid of the sub sometime this evening and we're scheduled to go alongside *Lexington* tomorrow morning to take on provisions. I'll contact *Lexington* and see about getting you on board. We may have to highline you over though. Ever been high-lined between two moving ships before?"

"Ahh, no Sir. This will be a first."

"It can be a little nerve-racking, but don't let it bother you. Chief Boatswain Sanders will take good care of you," Captain Feeney said with a mischievous grin.

That evening after evening chow, Stephens and several other *Kamey* bluejackets, including the two photographer wannabes he had met earlier, Lt. (jg) Larry Jason and BMSN Joe Wilson, were lounging on the fantail, enjoying the gentle rocking of the ship, drinking strong black coffee and watching a breathtaking sunset.

"Yowl!" Wilson yelled. "Can anything be more beautiful than a sunset at sea?"

"It's one hell of time to be without color film, I can tell you that." Stephens said.

"Here, have a roll of the world's best color slide film," Lt. Jason said, tossing a 20 exposure roll of Kodachrome to Stephens, "compliments of the ship's store."

"Hey, thanks lieutenant. I'll remember this."

"Kodachrome's really a good film, huh?" Wilson asked as Stephens quickly loaded the film into his Nikon."

"There's no better color film in the world," Ty answered. "Unfortunately, it has to be returned to Kodak for processing. But, if there's not a pressing time issue, its sharpness and vibrant color makes the wait well worth while."

"Hey, Ty," Lt. (jg) Jason said, addressing Stephens by his first name, "what do you think of the new Nikon F Photomic?"

"I really don't know that much about it. From what little

[86]

I have read about it though, it has one dynamite of an exposure meter and that will make it especially usual when shooting slides. Other than that, I don't see a lot of difference between it and the good old reliable Nikon F," Ty said holding up his own, well used Nikon F.

After another 30 minutes of chit chat Stephens stood up, fired off a couple more sunset frames and said, "Thanks for the hospitality guys. I've really enjoyed my stay aboard *Kamey* but I gotta get packed."

"You leaving?" Jason asked.

"Yeah, I'm being high-lined to the *Lexington* tomorrow and, hopefully from there I can get a hop back to Norfolk. See you," he said with a wave of his hand.

****

Stephens was standing on the port side of the torpedo deck getting a briefing on highline procedures from Chief Sanders when the warbling sound of the boatswain's pipe got their attention.

"Now the underway replenishment detail, man your stations. Petty Officer Stephens report to the bridge."

"We'll continue this later," the chief said, "you better hustle on up to the bridge."

"Good morning Petty Officer Stephens," Lt. Commander. Bolton said smiling. I believe the Captain has a little going away gift for you."

"Good morning Captain," Stephens said, coming to attention and snapping a salute."

[87]

"At ease, Stephens, at ease. Petty officer Stephens during your all too brief stay about *Kamey* the crew has eagerly accepted you as one of them. Therefore it is my pleasure to designate you an honorary *USS Kamey* crewmember," Captain Feeney said presenting Stephens with an honorary crewmember certificate, signed by both him and the executive officer.

"Preparing to go alongside *Lexington* Captain," the OOD interrupted.

"Very well, I have the con. Chief Sanders will be waiting for you," the Captain said, shaking Ty's hand. "Hope to see you again real soon. Good luck."

Returning to the torpedo deck the Navy photographer was handed a life jacket and told to set down in a metal and canvas contraption called a boatswain's chair.

"Enjoyed having you with us, Stephens," Chief Sanders said, checking to ensure that he was strapped in correctly. "Enjoy the ride."

Stepping back, Sanders gave a single to the line handlers and the boatswain's chair suddenly shot into the air and slowly moved upward and out over the raging water between the destroyer and carrier. A moment later the chair took a sudden plunge downward, stopping only three feet or so from the churning, watery trough produced by hundreds of tons of salt water trapped between the two ships.

"Ahhh shit! There go my cameras!" Stephens screamed, just as the chair snapped upward, leaving only his feet wet and slowly proceeded up a thirty degree incline toward the out stretched hands of a grinning *Lexington* line hander.

"Welcome aboard the Blue Ghost," the grinning sailor snickered helping Stephens out of the chair. "Captain said to escort you directly to the photo lab. How was the ride?"

"Terrifying," Stephens groaned, checking to ensure his camera gear was still intact. "I bet you guys get a real kick out transporting poor suckers like me between ships don't you?"

"Yeah, it is kind of fun. Especially when we get the ones who scream like little girls," the line handler chuckled.

Chapter 10

Tensions Mount

While *Kamey* and most of the *Lexington* ASW task group were saying their final farewells to *B-132,* the *USS Kennedy* was bearing down on the Lebanese freighter *Marcula*, which President Kennedy had chosen to be the first ship boarded. With darkness quickly descending over the area and not knowing how the freighter's Captain might respond, *Kennedy's* commanding officer decided it would be best to wait until morning before attempting to board.

After an all night vigil the *Kennedy* boarding party boarded the Lebanese ship without any resistance. After a thorough search the ship was cleared to continue its voyage to Cuba.

At about the same time that quarantine forces were completing their inspection of the *Marcula*, back in Washington the CIA Director was informing the president that several of the missiles deployed in Cuba were now fully operational and recommended that the security alert be upgraded to DEFCON-2

To make matters worse, a series of blunders had resulted in a U-2 reconnaissance plane straying off course and shot down over Russia; and a Navy RF-8A photo Crusader from VFP-62 had been fired upon as it made a low-level reconnaissance flight over Cuba.

Upon hearing the news at the White House the Secretary of Defense, fearing that the Soviet Union would interpret the U-2 flight as a reconnaissance mission prior to a nuclear strike yelled hysterically — "This probably means war with the Soviet Union!"

Maintaining a calm and controlled reaction President Kennedy simply remarked, "Well Bob, you know how it is, there is always some son of a bitch who doesn't get the word."

The following day, while considering their next move in the growing crisis, the Executive Committee of the National Security Council received still more alarming news. Another U-2 reconnaissance aircraft had been shot down. This one over Cuba by a surface-to-air missile, and had crashed on the eastern side of the island. The shoot down was interpreted by U.S. defense officials as a planned escalation of the situation by the Kremlin.

"It's time to stop screwing around," Air Force Chief of Staff, General Curtis LeMay demanded. "Let me turn my boys loose, Mr. President, and the Soviets will rue the day they ever thought about putting missiles in Castro country."

"Hold on General," the Secretary of State cautioned, "I just received this message from Ambassador Anatoly Dobrynin," he said reading the paper he had just been handed by an aide. "Mr. President, according to this, the order to launch a missile against one of our U-2s over Cuban did not come from Premier Khrushchev but from a soviet ground commander in Cuba; which, I might add, has Mr. Khrushchev worried that he may be losing control of his ground forces based in Cuba. Ambassador Dobrynin also assured me that the responsible officer has been relieved of duty and ordered back to Russia."

In an earlier meeting the president and the National Security Council had decided that if an American reconnaissance plane was shot down, the Air Force would retaliate by bombing the launch site. Now that it had happened, the Joint Chiefs, who had been pressing for permission to bomb Cuba, were anxious to get started.

"Mr. President, we must attack quickly," the Secretary of Defense insisted. "We've been fired on today. We're going to send in surveillance aircraft again tomorrow and without question, they are going to be fired on again. We can't just sit around, Mr. President, and wait for our aircraft to be shot out of the sky. We are prepared to attack Cuba and I believe we should attack quickly."

"No Bob, not yet. Let's hold off and see if another U-2 is shot at. If it is, then General LeMay, you can send in your bombers to take out the SAM sites. We all know that communications between the United States and the Soviet Union are sluggish at best; we need to give Premier Khrushchev time to respond. I don't want people saying I started World War III while the Soviet proposal to end the crisis was en route."

Privately, right from the beginning of the crisis, Kennedy and Khrushchev had been looking for ways to end the standoff before things got totally out of control. Communications between the two super powers however, travelled at a snail's pace, which was a major annoyance for both governments.

****

NAS Cecil Field
Jacksonville, Florida

"Commander, I have a bad feeling about this flight," Chief Photographer's Mate Randy Boyne said as he and VFP-62 Commanding Officer Commander Ron Johnson watched a flight of six Crusaders left off for still another low-level reconnaissance mission over Cuba.

"They know what they are doing chief. There are Fightin' Photos best. They'll be okay and they'll get the pictures. Make sure your guys have the Versamats QCed and ready to go. There will be an A-3 standing by to fly the film to Washington as soon as it's dry."

Within minutes of takeoff, two of the F8U-1P Crusaders declared in-flight emergencies and returned to base, the other four continued their mission and returned to Jacksonville where Chief Boyne and his photographers retrieved the photo Crusaders cameras and rushed the film to the lab for processing.

The flight wasn't without problems, however. Just as the Secretary of Defense had predicated, the photo birds encountered Cuban anti-aircraft fire the moment they roared in over the San Cristóbal and Sagua la Grande missile sites. One aircraft was hit, but managed to complete the mission and return to base.

****

The White House

The president and his advisors were studying Dobrynin's note and the latest VFP-62 photos, when a letter from the Soviet Premier arrived over a White House ticker.

Some members of the National Security Council speculated that hard-liners had pressured Khrushchev to take a more aggressive position and the letter was publicly broadcast in order to reduce communication delays. The broadcast, however, further raised the stakes. The two countries no longer had the luxury of private negotiations. Khrushchev wrote:

"Mr. President:
You are disturbed over Cuba. You say that this disturbs you because it is ninety miles by sea from the coast of the United States of America. But . . . you have placed destructive missile weapons, which we call offensive, in Turkey, literally next to us.
I therefore make this proposal: We are willing to remove from Cuba the means which you regard as offensive ...
Your representatives will make a declaration to the effect that the United States ... will remove its analogous means from Turkey.

And after that, persons entrusted by the United Nations Security Council could inspect on the spot the fulfillment of the pledges made."

"He's got us in a pretty good spot here," the President said. "I believe most people will regard this proposal as being very reasonable. What he's saying is; 'If you get yours out of Turkey, we'll get ours out of Cuba.'"

"In fact I think we'll find it very difficult to explain why we're invading Cuba to remove offending missiles, when we could have gotten the missiles out by simply making a deal to remove equally offending missiles from Turkey."

Still, the president concerned about political pressure, was worried about trading the removal of U.S. missiles from Turkey for the removal of Soviet missiles from Cuban and made his feelings clear to his advisors.

"I have an idea," the president's brother, Robert, said. "Let's assure Khrushchev that the United States will quietly remove its missiles from Turkey a few months after this crisis is over, but impress upon him that this cannot be part of a public deal."

"Great idea Bobby! You will meet with Ambassador Dobrynin tomorrow and tell him of our proposal," the president said. "And we'll give Dobrynin an ultimatum. If the Soviets do not remove those missiles from Cuban, we will remove them. And, Bobby, tell Dobrynin that a Soviet commitment is needed by tomorrow."

****

Moscow

Early Sunday morning, October 28, 1962 Premier Khrushchev was meeting with a circle of his closest advisers, informing them of President Kennedy's message and ultimatum he had received during the night, when a general entered the room with a message from the Soviet Ambassador in Washington.

President Kennedy was going to make an address to the nation at 5:00 p.m. Khrushchev feared the worst. Was the American President going to announce that an invasion of Cuba was already underway? Khrushchev's advisors suggested that the Premier draft a letter with the utmost urgency and hope that it would reach Kennedy prior to 5:00 p.m., Washington time.

"Esteemed Mr. President:" Khrushchev wrote,
"I have received your message of October 27, 1962. I express my satisfaction and gratitude for the sense of proportion and understanding of the responsibility borne by you at present for the preservation of peace throughout the world...
In order to complete with greater speed the liquidation of the conflict — the Soviet Government — in addition to previously issued instructions on the cessation of further work at building sites for the weapons, has issued a new order on the dismantling of the weapons which you describe as "offensive," and their crating.

Khrushchev's message effectively ended the crisis but was welcomed in Washington with mixed reaction. While most of the Executive Committee was relieved that a war had been avoided others, especially the Joint Chiefs, thought the announcement might be a ploy by the Soviets to gain more time.

"I don't trust those Commie sons-of-bitches," General LeMay said. "I still say we go in and take them out."

The President, however, was sure the response was genuine. "A nuclear war will destroy both nations," he told LeMay and the other staff members, and immediately drafted a response to Khrushchev which was broadcast over the Voice of America:

*"I welcome Chairman Khrushchev's statesmanlike deci-
sion to stop building bases in Cuba, dismantling offensive weapons and returning them to the Soviet Union. . .
I think that you and I, with our heavy responsibilities for
the maintenance of peace, were aware that developments
were approaching a point where events could have be-
come unmanageable. So I welcome this message and
consider it an important contribution to peace."*

Tensions eased with the receipt of Khrushchev message,
but the ordeal was still far from over. Terms of a formal
agreement between the two superpowers still had to be
hammered out. During the course of the final negotiations Castro, who felt betrayed, tried to halt the removal
and inspection of the missiles but eventually, with the
help of the U.N., the Cuban dictator backed down and
the two sides reached an agreement. A U.N. inspection
team was assigned to monitor the removal of the missiles
and the demolition of the missile bases in Cuba. Then,
the Soviet Navy shipped the missiles back to the
U.S.S.R. The missiles were sent back on the decks of the
ships so that American reconnaissance planes could
count the missiles and make sure that all had been re-
moved.

Chapter 11

USS Kamey

While Washington and Moscow were rejoicing, the American fleet enforcing the blockade was still diligently caring out their duties.

The *USS Kamey* had been performing plane guard duty for the *Lexington* for most of the day and was taking up a new position two miles off the stern of the carrier when the squawk box suddenly came alive.

"Bridge-Sonar: Contact bearing zero five zero!"

"Sonar-Bridge: What've you got?"

Bridge-Sonar: Appears to be a Foxtrot.

"I've got the Conn," Bolton growled taking control from the OOD. "Right full rudder, turns for eighteen knots. Set Condition One Anti-submarine."

"What's up XO?" Captain Feeney said bursting through the pilot house door, just as the OOD yelled out, "Captain's on the bridge."

"Sonar contact Sir, bearing zero five zero. Sonar identifies it as a Foxtrot. You don't think it's that clown we let go yesterday do you Captain?"

"Couldn't be. There is no way he could have gotten his engines repaired and returned to this position in this short amount of time. There has to be more than one out there."

"Comm-Bridge: Contact *Lexington*. See if the ASW helicopters have picked up a contact."

Bridge-Comm: No contact by ASW birds. They're starting a new search.

****

Soviet Submarine B-52

Unbeknown to any ship in the Hunter Killer Group the new contact was having many of the same problems which had earlier forced *B-132* to the surface. Actually all four of the Northern Fleet Foxtrot submarines which had set sail for Cuba on October 1, had encountered serious problems. One, the *B-36* was forced to perform surgery more than 300 feet under water while Hurricane Ella was whipping up mountainous waves on the surface, after a crewmember came down with appendicitis.

Like a scene from an old World War II movie, The *B-36* crew cleaned a wardroom table with alcohol and the doctor, assisted by a crewmember, successfully performed the operation.

B-52 however, the submarine SO1 Jack Reed, *Kamey's* senior sonar man was now tracking, came closest to suffering the same problems encountered by *B-132*. During the height of Hurricane Ella, *B-52's* skipper, Captain

Valentin Savisky, had made a desperate attempt to re-charge his batteries. The storm seriously damaged the submarine's snorkel and ruptured deck hatch seals, allowing saltwater to flow into the submarine covering the diesel cooling systems with seawater. From that point on the diesel engines and electric compressors took turns malfunctioning causing the crew to endure stifling hot conditions averaging between 122 and 140 degrees while fighting to save their ship.

As *B-52* approached the East Coast of the United States, radio intercepts indicated that the submarine had been detected by an American ASW task force.

Captain Savisky suddenly found himself in water about 1,800 feet deep and far too warm for comfort. The tropics began to have their effect and the necessity to remain submerged quickly rendered the air inside the submarine hot and stale. All efforts to elude the American destroyer proved to be unsuccessful in the face of the overwhelming force of an eight ship American task group just above.

****

USS Kamey

"Bridge-Sonar: No doubt about it Captain, it's a Fox-trot.

"Weapons-Bridge: Prepare to drop grenades."

"XO, let's get this bastard on the surface before Washington gets word of it and orders us to hold off until the *Kennedy* or some other ship named for some bureaucrats relative arrives."

"You got it Captain I'm going below and personally take charge of bringing this Commie asshole to the surface," Lt. Commander. Bolton said bolting out on-to the open bridge.

B-52 was rattled with active sonar pings and the customary three-grenade explosion signals ordering the submarine to surface. Within moments of the *Kamey* grenade explosions other destroyers assigned to the Hunter-Killer Group converged on the scene while H-3 Sea King ASW helicopters from the carriers *Lexington* and *Randolph* circled overhead and dropped sonobuoys into the water in still another attempt to communicate with the Soviet submarine.

****

Soviet Submarine B-52

Tension among the crew of *B-52* intensified. They could hear the explosions through the hull, leaving most of the sub's crew to believe they were being depth charged. Air inside the submarine grew worse and blue indicator lights illuminated the propulsion compartment indicating that the batteries desperately needed a recharge.

Realizing that the odds were totally against him, Savisky gave the order to surface. Not knowing what to expect and angry about the entire situation, Savisky ordered the nuclear torpedo *B-52* was carrying in the forward torpedo room, to be loaded into a torpedo tube just before surfacing. He didn't know what to expect and he certainly wasn't going to take any chances.

The Captain signaled his intention to surface with his active sonar in conformity with international rules. At precisely 1700 hours *B-52* surfaced smack in the middle of a circle of surface ships and hovering helicopters. The sudden surge of fresh air made Savisky and several of his officers woozy as they filled their lungs on ascending to the sail bridge. As *B-52's* senior officers watched the display of naval might on the surface, radio operators worked furiously to communicate with Northern Fleet Headquarters. It took nearly 40 minutes before they made contact and another twenty minutes before *B-52* received a reply.

"Captain Savisky, you are ordered to dive immediately to a depth you deem necessary to escape the American Task Force. You will then evade and head for Bermuda. We are not at war with the Americans and they have no right to detain your ship.

"Repeat, the Soviet Union IS NOT at war with the United States, and B-52 should avoid starting one at all costs."

It would take at least a full 18 hours to completely recharge his batteries before any attempt could be made to follow Northern Fleet's instructions. As the sluggish batteries were brought back to life, Savisky was further surprised to find that another aircraft carrier — *USS* Randolph — and her escorts, ten ships in all, had joined the *USS Kamey* and *USS Lexington.* To try and

evade such a heavily armed armada was beyond im-
agination.

There was little Savisky could do while waiting for the
batteries to charge so he put his men to work performing routine ship's chores and allowed the crew to go
topside in small groups to get some long overdue fresh
air and watch ASW aircraft drop scores of sonobuoys
to keep track of the submarines every movement.

For Captain Savisky and his men being surrounded by
the American Navy was a humiliating experience.
American sailors wearing summer trousers, blue shirts,
and white hats consumed cool drinks, smiled, played
Yankee Doodle, danced around and took pictures of
the dirty, sweaty Soviet submarine crew gulping in
clean fresh air.

B-52's senior officers were further humiliated by the
gesture of American sailors tossing bottles of Coca-
Cola and packs of cigarettes to the Russians, despite
the fact that the Russian sailors eagerly snapped up
every cigarette and soda tossed to them.

In spite of a feeling of intense irritation with the Americans, the message from Northern Fleet Headquarters,
made it perfectly clear, that other than perhaps hurt
pride, there were no hostiles between the Soviet Union
and the United States. With that thought uppermost in
his mind, Captain Savisky ordered the forward torpedo
room to remove the nuclear torpedo and return it to its
storage rack, relieving the apprehension felt by many
of *B-52's* officers and senior non-commissioned officers.

Captain Valentin Savisky was a professional and highly dedicated submarine commander and no one onboard had any doubt that, if attacked, their Captain would never have waited for a special order to launch the torpedo. He would have acted on his own initiative.

****

USS Kamey

"That thing is a hell of a lot bigger than I thought it was," Lt. Commander. Bolton said to Captain Feeney, staring at the 294-foot, 2,475-ton Soviet submarine through *Kamey's* "Big Eye" telescope mounted on the starboard open bridge from a quarter-mile away. "She's actually a good looking boat."

"Yeah, it does have some nice lines," Captain Feeney agreed.

"Captain now that it's on the surface can we give the crew a break and secure from general quarters?"

"Sure, let them unwind a little but let's not secure from GQ entirely. Set Modified Condition ZEBRA, that will give the crew a little more freedom of movement and let the ship air out a little. I don't believe we have anything to fear from our Russian friend here, but we can't totally discount that possibility either.

"Let as many people below deck as possible come topside to get a look at this. It's not every day that they are going to see a Soviet submarine on the surface surrounded by half of the Atlantic Fleet. You know, Paul, I think we let our roving photographer get away a little too soon," *Kamey's* commanding officer said, shaking his head. "Yep, without a doubt, this is a true Kodak moment."

****

Soviet Submarine B-52

When the battery recharge concluded, *B-52* began moving slowly on the surface toward Bermuda.

"Comrade Captain the carriers are withdrawing" the radio operator reported. "The carriers have been instructed to leave four surface ships to escort us to Bermuda. Intercepted communication further indicates that surveillance aircraft are to track *B-52* until we are completely out of the area."

For the next few hours *B-52* proceeded on a steady easterly course then just past midnight, between regular floodlight illuminations from the escort ships, Savitsky gave the order to dive.

"Make your depth 350 feet; come to course south one-eight-zero make revolutions for fourteen knots."

Fifteen minutes later when the destroyers' search lights again swept the area, *B-52* had vanished. Three hours later, satisfied that he had given the Americans the slip

Captain Savitsky resurfaced and informed Northern Fleet Headquarters of his escape.

****

USS Kamey

"Bridge-Sonar:

"Go ahead sonar"

"We've lost him Captain," SO1 Reed said. "Last contact one-eight-zero, heading out of our operating area.

"Sonar-Bridge: Stay alert and let me know if you pick up any further contact."

"Permission to leave the bridge Sir. I want to make sure all the depth charges have been disarmed."

"Permission granted, XO. The last thing we need is for 200 pounds of high explosives in an armed depth charge to go off. Oh, Paul, while you're down below get a reading from Chief Dunlap on how the fire room crews are holding up. I know it's hotter than hell down there and he is short handed in both fire rooms.

On the main deck Bolton found his old childhood friend Chief Boiler Tender Maxwell Dunlap, leaning on a life rail, gazing out at the choppy blue-green water.

"How's it going Max," the XO asked. "I assume you have everything under control below."

"Hey, XO. Going as well as can be expected I guess. Hotter than a July day back home down in the holes and

[106]

my snipes are working six on and two off. They are holding out, Paul, but I don't know how much longer they can take it. Without question these are some of the best boiler techs I've ever worked with. But, Sir, the hours, the heat and being at battle stations for hours on end is getting to them. Hell, it's getting to me too."

"It's getting to all of us Max; it's been what, two weeks now, since we got underway? And we've been at GQ for damned near the whole time. All I can tell you old friend, is hang in there. Hopefully, one way or the other, it'll all be over real soon."

"What are you guys hearing on the bridge, Paul?"

"Not much more than what the President said the other night. We had a U-2 shot down over Cuba and several Navy reconnaissance aircraft have encountered anti-aircraft fire from Cuban defense forces, but the read we're getting is that both sides are looking for an 'honorable' solution... what the hell ever that means. Anyway Max, and you can relay this to your men, from the radio traffic we're picking up I don't think the United States or the Russians are willing to launch World War Three over a shit bag island like Cuba. But, that is just my opinion."

"You've always had pretty good insight when it comes to politics, Paul, so I'll take your word for it — and hope like hell you're right," the Chief Boiler Tender, snickered. "Guess I better back down in the hole. See you, later, sir."

"Yeah, see you chief. If we hear anything new I'll let you know. Oh, by the way, we'll be refueling from the tanker *Algol* tomorrow at 1500.

[107]

"Max, after this shit's all over with, why don't we go home for a while, go fishing… maybe get in a little hunting."

"Sounds damn good to me. The Southern Appalachians this time of year would feel mighty good after being cooped up down here," the chief said as his head disappeared down the hatch leading to fire room number one.

"Been one of hell of week, huh, chief," Ensign Randolph Harris, the R Division Officer said propping his feet up on the edge of the chief's desk in the Shipfitter shop.

"Yea, I suppose you could say that Mr. Harris," Chief Jeff Curtis grunted. "Fortunately no one has shot at us yet. I don't mind telling you sir, those damn submarines we've been playing around with scare the hell out of me. My oldest brother was a Boatswain's Mate on board the light cruiser *Juneau* when it was torpedoed and sunk by a Japanese submarine during the Battle of Guadalcanal."

"Did he survive?"

"He did, thank God. But the stories he used to tell about the sinking, spending two days in shark infested waters and nearly dying of thirst; burned an unforgettable image in my mind. Yes sir, the very idea of being torpedoed by a submarine scares the shit out of me."

"Well chief, from what Lt. Slack, the ASW officer, tells me there may not be too much to worry about. According to Charlie, that last boat we were tracking has completely left our operating area. He suspects it received orders to return to base. Course that may have been because of some mechanical problem, but at least it is no longer a threat to us."

"Well now that is good to know Mr. Harris, but how many others are still down there nosing around just waiting for us to let our guard down?"

"There may very well be a few more down there Chief, so let's thank our blessings that *Kamey* is under the command of the two best anti-submarine officers in the fleet. If it comes to a shoot out between a commie sewer pipe and *Kamey*, my money is on Commander Feeney and Lt. Commander Bolton.

"No argument from me about that. What concerns me is the type of weapons the Soviets may be carrying. Let's face it Mr. Harris, if *Kamey* or any of the other ships out here, finds itself in the crosshairs of a nuclear torpedo — which they are rumored to have — we're all history; no matter who has the helm."

"I wouldn't sweat that Chief. We were told in OCS that some Soviet submarines do carry nuclear missiles, but nuclear torpedoes? I've never heard of such a thing. Hell, we don't even have nuclear torpedoes."

"All due respect, Mr. Harris, but I'm sure there's a hell of a lot they didn't tell you at knife and folk school. I'm not saying Soviet submarines actually do carry nuclear-tipped torpedoes. I'm simply saying they 'may' have them. And as far as American subs being equipped with nuke fish...well, Mr. Harris, I wouldn't go and bet the farm against that either."

[109]

"You are probably right chief, I wouldn't bet against us having them either. Say Chief, you ever been to Cuba, other than Gitmo, I mean?"

"Couple of times matter of fact. Course that was long before Castro."

"What was it like?"

"Back in the Batista days Havana was a great liberty port. Good restaurants, duty-free shopping, a casino on every street corner and great beaches. Tourists from all over the United States, Canada and Europe flocked to Havana for vacations in those days, especially during the winter. And cathouses ... my God, they were everywhere.

"Hold on a minute, Chief, if Cuban was such a great place how did Castro manage to come to power?"

"Havana itself was a wealthy, thriving city, thanks to Batista's lucrative relationship with the American mafia and large multinational corporations. Outside of Havana, however, it was a totally different story. Under Batista, Cuban, as it is now, was of one the poorest countries in the Western world. So when Castro came along spouting his revolutionary propaganda the Cuban people welcomed him as their savior. Little could they have known that in just a couple of years their lives would change from bad to worse."

"When was the last time you were in Havana?"

"Let's see...that would be nineteen fifty-seven, aboard the *USS Graham County (LST-1176)*, two years before Castro took over. Actually met Bob Hope in a casino there."

"No shit! You met Bob Hope at a casino in Havana Cuba?"

"Sure did. Four of us from the old flat-bottom *Graham County* had been 'sight-seeing' and stopped to grab a bite to eat and try our luck with the slots before going back to the ship. We had no more than set down when a waiter brought over four beers and said they were compliments of the party across the room. We looked in the direction the waiter was pointing and lo-and-behold if it wasn't the King of Comedy himself, raising a class in salute."

"Wow! That's really something. With famous entertainers buying sailors drinks, I can see why you say Havana was a great liberty port. Damn, looks like I came along a few years too late," the young ensign said dropping his feet to the deck and standing.

"Your turn will come, Sir. After this is all over you will have a start on some damn good sea stories of your own. Oh by the way, before I forget, I had that acetylene bottle bracket that broke during the storm replaced and all the others were inspected and are in good shape."

****

Soviet Submarine K-153

Captain Second Rank Ivan Mayakovsky slowly brought the Golf class submarine *K-153* to periscope depth fifty miles East of Cape Canaveral, Florida. After taking a careful look at the Florida coastline, he slowly rotated the periscope 180 degrees, carefully scanning the surface and skies above his position. The sonar operator promptly reported two American destroyers ten miles off the port bow, sailing a southwesterly course, apparently

oblivious to *K-153's* presence. Unlike his fellow undersea warriors on board the Foxtrots that had blindly
prowled these same waters mere hours before, Captain
Mayakovsky was fully aware of the current tension between the United States and the Soviet Union. His orders, which had been locked in a tiny safe in the state
room of the Political Officer until ten minutes earlier,
were direct and to the point. *K-153* was to take up a position approximately midway between Miami and Jacksonville, Florida and stand by, undetected, for further instructions.

"Down scope," Mayakovsky ordered, "Come right seven
degrees, prepare to load missiles."

K-153, like all early Soviet Golf class submarines, was
equipped with missile lunching tubes and carried thirteen
R-11FM liquid-propellant single-stage missiles, which
could be fitted with a nuclear warhead. The navigator,
Warrant Officer Alek Volkov programmed one nuclear-
tipped R-11FM with coordinates for Miami and a second
for Jacksonville."

Remaining undetected was already proving to be a difficult task. A U.S. Navy P-2H Neptune Maritime Patrol an
anti-Submarine aircraft flying out of Naval Air Station
Jacksonville had already detected *K-153's* presence and
relayed its position to a *USS Essex* based S2F anti-
submarine aircraft.

****

USS Kamey

For the first time since their abrupt departure from Mayport, *Kamey* sailors had enjoyed a restful night without the bonging of the general quarters alarm and many, who normally worked below deck, were lounging about the weather deck taking advantage of the late October South Atlantic sun to regain the tan they had lost during seven months the Mediterranean.

BM2 Donald Patton and BT2 Charlie Pate, both of whom would have refueling station responsibilities when Kamey went alongside the attack cargo ship *USS Algol* were spread out on the helicopter deck, drinking strong black coffee, smoking Pall Malls and discussing the upcoming refueling operation. Patton would be in charge of the line handling crew securing the two ships together and supervise the receiving of the fuel lines. Pate and his men would be responsible for attaching the fuel hoses to *Kamey's* fueling trunk and disconnecting the hose when the refueling operation was complete. In addition to topping off the fuel tanks both veteran destroyermen where hoping that maybe, just maybe, they might receive mail, which was always a big deal for sailors at sea.

"Know anything about the *Algol*? Pate asked.

"Nope, just another floating gas station, we go alongside and they fill us up. Never bother to check the tires or wash the windshield though," Patton laughed at his attempt at humor.

Commissioned in July 1944, four months after *Kamey*

had entered service; *Algol* had won two battle stars for combat service in World War II and five more during the Korean War for performing the always dangerous task of supplying fuel, ammunition and other war fighting supplies to American and allied warships.

"Donald," Pate said, "unlike those of us who slave away in the bowels of this bucket of bolts, you're up there with the brass a good bit of the time, have you gotten a feel for what's really going on out here?"

"There's a lot of scuttlebutt, Charlie, but it's really hard to pin anything down. All messages from DesRonSix, or the admiral, over on the bird farm, go directly to the skipper or XO. Even the OOD seldom gets a look at them. Of course the geeks in CIC see all incoming message traffic, but their lips are permanently sealed."

"So what's the scuttlebutt?"

"Well, according to the latest rumor the Russians are about ready to remove their missiles from Cuba. But, the high flying recon planes are reporting that ships with missiles aboard are still inbound for Cuba and show no signs of stopping or turning around."

"So besides looking for submarines, we may soon be firing at Soviet freighters?"

"That could very well be, old buddy. And, if the XO has his way any Soviet freighter that doesn't stop will be blown out of the water without as much as a 'by your leave sir', and checked for contraband later."

"You got that right. Every time I encounter that crusty old seadog I expect him to be carrying a cutlass and wearing an eye patch."

"Ha-ha; you've got the XO pegged alright. Yeah, can't you just see him with an eye patch swinging from the yardarm, with a saber between his teeth, yelling 'NEVER GIVE UP THE SHIP, ME LADDIES.' "

Their psychoanalysis of *Kamey's* executive officer was suddenly interrupted by the warbling of the boatswain's pipe.

"Now set the underway refueling detail. All assigned personnel, man your refueling stations. The smoking lamp is out throughout the ship."

"That's us old buddy, time to earn our keep," Petty Officer Patton, said. "Catch you later."

Lingering a couple minutes longer, the boiler tech shaded his eyes with his right hand and stared at the 459-foot attack cargo ship riding low in the water two miles ahead.

"Looks like she's fully loaded," he said to Chief Sanders who had just walked up.

"Yeah, she's carrying a full load alright, probably just left port."

"Great," said Patton, "maybe she will have some mail for us."

Refueling at sea always created an environment of squirminess for bridge personnel and Captain Feeney, the veteran that he was, certainly wasn't immune from the feeling as he carefully watched the distance between the *Kamey* and the attack cargo ship slowly decrease.

"Slow ahead" he ordered the engine order telegraph operator. "Watch your helm," he said to the helmsman as *Kamey* slowly moved alongside the supply ship.

"Standby to receive shot line," Chief Boatswain Larry Sanders shouted, sending personnel in the immediate vicinity scurrying for cover as a lead projectile with a line attached was fired from the *Algol* .

Rushing from their hiding places as soon as the padded 10-ounce lead projectile landed on deck, deck division personnel snagged the line, attached to a two-inch span wire, and hauled the fueling hose aboard.

"Hose attached, BT2 Charlie Pate said to the phone talker who then relayed the message to the bridge. Within moments the life blood of Kamey's propulsion system; thick, black fuel oil began flowing into the destroyer's fuel tanks.

While Pate and his crew stood guard over the refueling operation, back on the helo deck, Chief Sanders watched closely as four seamen wrestled a cargo net, filled with spare parts, fresh fruit and other miscellaneous cargo, including an orange-colored canvas sack labeled, U.S. Mail onto the deck. One sailor, BM3 Jake Delosa, a Navy brat born and raised in the largest Navy town in the world ... Norfolk, Virginia, unhooked the transfer line from the net and the others dragged it clear.

"STAND BY FOR BREAK AWAY!" the ship's speakers suddenly blared. Pate glanced at his watch, 1555. "I think we've just set a record for underway refueling — 55-minutes flat, he boosted as the span wire retreated back toward the *Algol*.

"Starboard five degrees, set speed for 15 knots" Feeney ordered, as *Kamey* gradually pulled away from the tanker.

"I've done this hundreds of times," said Lt. Commander. Bolton, "and I'm always in awe of the whole concept of underway replenishment. Look at her," he said pointing at the *Algol* slowly steaming away to the northeast at 10 knots.

"She's a supermarket, gas station, supply center and ammo depot all rolled into one."

"That she is XO," Captain Feeney replied "it's moments like this when you realize the true potential of American sea power. It makes the old heart throb and chest swell with pride to be a part of the greatest Navy on earth," the destroyer skipper said thumping his chest. "Yes sir it makes you proud."

****

"Bridge-Radar: Contact two miles off the port quarter, bearing south, southeast, eight knots.

"Radar-Bridge: Can you ID it?"

"Bridge-Radar: Affirmative Sir. It's the Soviet registered freighter *Kasimov*. ASW aircraft from *Lake Champlain* reports what appear to be missile containers on the main deck."

[117]

"All ahead full," the Captain ordered. "Sound general quarters."

Instantly the BONG, BONG, BONG of the general alarm sent *Kamey* sailors scurrying for their battle stations.

"Wonder what the hell's going on now?" SF2 Andy Warden said to no one in particular as he assumed his position as Repair Leader of Repair Station Two, in the forward section of the ship.

"It ain't no submarine this time … don't hear none of that damn ear splitting pinging," a large black sailor from Mobile, Alabama, grumbled.

"If you don't get that helmet on, Wells, the pinging of sonar is gonna be the least of your worries. If those five-inchers start firing, those lights yonder," Warden said pointing to a series of overhead light fixtures, "are gonna be bouncing off your damn hard head."

"These things hurt my head," Wells protested, throwing the metal helmet on the deck "I'll take my chances."

"Comm-Bridge: Advise the approaching freighter that it is entering a restricted area."

"Bridge-Comm: She refuses to reverse course, sir."

"Mr. Waters," Captain Feeney instructed the communications officer, "bring her up on ship-to-ship."

"This is U.S. Navy warship *Kamey*. You are entering a restricted zone. Reverse course immediately. I say again, reverse course immediately or you will be fired upon."

"She's not slowing down, Captain," the duty officer said, watching the ship through his binoculars.

"Signal her by flashing light and flags. Then if she fails to reverse course we open fire," Feeney told the executive officer.

Several minutes went by without any indication that the Soviet freighter was going to slow down or reserve course.

"Mounts one and two standby to fire," Lt. Commander. Bolton said to the Weapons Officer.

"Bridge-Weapons: Mounts One and Two loaded and ready to fire."

"She's proceeding on course, sir" the OOD said.

"Weapons-Bridge: Put a warning shot across her bow."

The entire ship shuddered as the forward 5in/38 naval gun of Mount Two belched a long plume of fire and smoke, sending a 54-pound projectile streaming over the Soviet freighter's bow.

"Damn!" screamed the two-hundred pound sailor from Mobile, as an overhead light fixture exploded, spewing glass and metal particles into his scalp and face.

"You shithead!" Warden shouted "I told you to put your helmet on. Get the corpsman up here," he yelled to the sound-powered phone talker. "Evans, see what you can do about getting that bleeding under control while we're waiting for doc," he ordered another member of Repair Two. "If I see as much as a loose helmet strip on the rest of you assholes I'll put you on report. You're at battle stations for Christ's sake and this is no damn drill. STAY ALERT!"

"Soviet freighter *Kasimov*. This is U.S. Navy destroyer *Kamey*. Turn around now. The next round will be a direct hit."

"Mount Two stand by to take out her rudder," Feeney said calmly.

"Captain, she's turning," the XO shouted. "By God, the commie bastard's turning skipper. I didn't think he would be dumb enough to screw with this here old tin can."

"Take up a position a thousand yards off her stern," Feeney directed the helmsman. Set speed for ten knots.

"Paul we'll stay with her until she is twenty miles outside the line. I'm going down to the wardroom and grab a sandwich. Call me if she changes course."

Aye, aye sir. Steady as she goes helmsman."

****

[120]

Washington
"Sunday October, 28

Just prior to noon Soviet Ambassador Dobrynin arrived at the Justice Department to extend Khrushchev's best wishes to the President and his brother Bobby. Later that afternoon Secretary of State Dean Rusk held a press conference and cautioned the American people against gloating over the Soviet decision to remove its missiles from Cuban. "If there is a debate, a rivalry, a contest going on in the Kremlin over how to play this situation," the Secretary warned, "we don't want to strengthen the hands of those in Moscow who wanted to play this another way." The Secretary of State also pointed out that because of inspections and other pending issues the crisis was far from being settled.

****

Havana, Cuba

In Cuba, Castro was furious. His first notification of the Moscow/Washington agreement came not from any official source, but a radio news report beamed in from Miami.

"Cuba has been betrayed by the Soviets," Castro fumed during a meeting with his own advisors. "That fat pig, Khrushchev, never once asked for our opinion," he complained to his brother and second in command, Raúl. "Khrushchev and Kennedy are in this together. They are plotting Cuban's future without bothering to consult Cuba."

Castro was convinced that an invasion of the island nation by the United States was imminent and angrily dictated a letter to Khrushchev demanding a preemptive strike on the U.S. In the meantime all Cuban anti-aircraft weapons were ordered to fire on any U.S. aircraft flying over Cuban air space, whereas in the past they had been ordered to fire only on groups of two or more aircraft.

The Cuban "president for life" was especially upset that certain issues of interest to Cuba, such as the status of Guantanamo, were never addressed. Any international agreement concerning Cuban, Castro wrote in a letter to Khrushchev, should have included an immediate end to the economic blockade against Cuba; an end to all subversive activities carried out from the United States against Cuba; a halt of attacks on Cuba carried out from the U.S. military bases by Cuban exiles in Puerto Rico; the cessation of all aerial and naval reconnaissance flights in Cuban airspace and waters; and the return of Guantanamo naval base to Cuba.

Unbeknown to either of the Castro brothers, however, was the simple fact, that Khrushchev didn't have time to inform his ally of his decision to remove the missiles from Cuba. It had been made painfully clear to Premier Nikita Khrushchev that the U.S. Strategic Air Command was airborne and ready to launch a nuclear strike on the Soviet Union and Cuban, on a moment's notice. In addition to the airborne forces, PGM-19 Jupiter intermediate range ballistic missiles, targeting the Soviet Union, were standing by in Italy and Turkey. An extra lethal punch was added by the fact that the ballistic missile submarines *George Washington* and *Ethan Allen*, capable of launching 16 Polaris missiles were on station less than a thousand miles off shore from the Soviet Union.

Both President John F. Kennedy and Premier Nikita Khrushchev: and their respective governments had come to the same conclusion: Cuba simply wasn't worth the assured destruction of two great nations.

****

USS *Kamey*

It had been two days since *Kamey* had made contact with the Soviet freighter *Kasimov,* which was now steaming on a northeasterly course well outside the quarantine line. Life aboard *Kamey* had returned to a semi-normal routine of modified general quarters, watch standing and long periods of boredom. Despite the fact that a mail sack had been included in the cargo received from the *USS Algol* during the last refueling operation it had remained locked in the ship's cubbyhole of a post office during *Kamey's* encounter with the *Kasimov.* A slight reprieve from the boredom was provided by a brief 1mc announcement.

"Now mail call, mail call! All division mail petty officers lay to the post office."

"It's 'bout damn time McCutheon got off his lazy ass and distributed the mail," complained BMSN Joe Wilson.

"Wilson, are you really that dumb or is it just an act?" BM2 Donald Patton asked. "Just how in the hell was Mc supposed to get the mail sorted when the ship was at general quarters? I swear, I don't know what this man's Navy is coming too with imbeciles like you wearing the uniform."

[123]

Postal Clerk Second Class Cas McCutheon from Blue-
field, West Virginia and Hospitalman First Class Bill
Fleming, from the small town of Max Meadows, Virginia, were literally one of a kind on board *Kamey*. Due to
limited space on small warships many of the "conven-
ience features" found on larger ships, such as fully
staffed hospitals, postal facilities and ships stories; were
limited. Sailors in need of medical care relied strictly on
HM1 Fleming and those wanting to buy postage stamps
or purchase a money order depended on PC2
McCutheon.

"Well now! Looks like we're famous," Chief Curtis said,
browsing through a copy of *Navy Times* which had come
aboard in the mail sack from the *Algol*.

"How's that?" Chief Boatswain's Mate Sanders asked as
he and several other chief petty officers, grabbing some
well deserved rest in the Chiefs Quarters, looked up.

"'Member that shutter checker we had on board for a
while? ... well a butch of the pictures he took are here in
the *Navy Times*."

"Let me see that," said Chief Boiler Tender Maxwell
Dunlap. "Well I'll be damned. That kid done a damn
good job. I wonder if the skipper's seen this yet?" he
said pushing away from the table and snatching a shipboard phone from its cradle.

"Afternoon Captain, Max Dunlap here," Dunlap was one
of the few enlisted men aboard the ship who never
feared making direct contract with the commanding officer. "Did you get a copy of the latest *Navy Times*?

Seems that fotog we had on board has done went and told the whole world how great the *Kamey* is."

"Yeah, Max I did. Commander Bolton and I were just looking at it. Think I'll write his commanding officer and recommend a citation."

"After the *Kennedy* fiasco this is just the morale booster we needed," Bolton said. "Maybe now the crew will feel that we're appreciated after all. Damn good headline, the executive officer said proudly."

"Mayport-based Destroyer USS Kamey Forces Soviet Submarine to Surface"

The banner headline on the front page of the Navy wide newspaper shouted, followed by a three column photo of the Soviet submarine *B-132* breaking the surface of the water, framed by *Kamey* sailors crowding the bow. On the inside was a story of how and why the submarine had surfaced, and the role *Kamey* had played in the operation.

"I'll never say anything bad 'bout shutter clickers again," proclaimed BT2 Charlie Pate, "that ole boy made us look good. I bet the *Kennedy* is having a shit hemorrhage right 'bout now. Hot damn, I would love to see their faces when they read this," he said, slapping his knee.

"Amen to that" several voices on the mess deck rang out in unison. "That will teach those credit grabbing assholes a lesson."

****

"Contact," Sonar man First Class Allen Jackson said into the mouthpiece on his helmet. Seated at the sonar console behind the cockpit of the Sikorsky H-3 Sea King from Anti-Submarine Squadron Five (HS-5) the helicopter's senior operator's eyes was fixed on a tiny, slowly moving blimp on the console screen. "No doubt about it Sir," he told the pilot, it's a submarine."

"Can you ID it yet?" the pilot, Ensign Marvin Repass asked.

"Working on it Sir." After making several quick adjustments to his sound equipment and consulting a thick book, Jackson was ready to confirm the near motionless submerged vessel.

"It's a Golf class, Sir; 2700 tons, diesel-electric propulsion, speed 12-14 knots submerged, and carries three R-21 missiles. Sir!" Jackson yelled into his helmet mike, "according to the book, that thing is probably armed with an SS-N-5 Serb Missile with a one megaton warhead; range of 750-900 nautical miles. Mr. Repass that is one dangerous boat we have down there."

"I'm on it Sonar," Ensign Repass said twisting dials on the helicopter's radio. "Home Plate: Sea King Five-Five over."

"Sea King Five-Five: Home Plate over."

"Home Plate we're tracking a Golf class boat. Believed to be the *K-153* and possibility armed with nuclear weapons."

"Stay with it, Five-Five. A fully armed S2-F from VS-32 is en route from *Lake Champlain*. Destroyer *USS Kamey* also in area and will assume overall ASW command. Remain on station and maintain contact until S-2 arrives on scene."

****

K-153

"Captain, sonobuoys in the water, fore and aft." an excited sonar operator announced as Captain Second Rank Mayakovsky grabbed the handles of the periscope.

"Up scope," Mayakovsky ordered. "Where did the sonobuoys come from?" the Captain asked.

"An ASW helicopter dropped them Sir," *K-153's* executive officer answered. "It seemed to come out of nowhere. Should we go deeper and try to evade Captain?"

"NO!" exclaimed the Political Officer. "Your orders, Captain, are to remain on station and await further instructions."

"Anti-submarine aircraft directly overhead," Captain Mayakovsky said nonchalantly as the peered through the periscope. "Here, have a look," he said to his number two.

"It's an S2-F anti-submarine aircraft, Captain. The S2-F is armed with bombs, missiles and torpedoes."

"What would you have us do, comrade," Mayakovsky asked the Political Officer, "remain on station and be blown out of the water?"

"Surface contact, Captain," the sonar operator shouted before the Political Officer had a chance to respond to Captain Mayakovsky's question.

"It's an American destroyer, Sir."

****

USS Kamey

Bridge-Sonar: Submarine contact five miles, depth 70 feet.

"GENERAL QUARTERS! GENERAL QUARTERS! Set ASW Condition One."

Sonar-Bridge: What's his speed?"

"Barely moving sir, 'bout five knots.

"Bridge-CIC: radio contact from S2-F anti-submarine aircraft."

"Pipe him through to the bridge," Captain Feeney instructed.

"This is *USS Kamey.* What is your status?" Feeney said into the radio.

"*Kamey;* this is VS-32 aircraft zero-zero-seven. Positive contact. Golf class submarine at periscope depth. Communication buoy is in the water. No response."

"Aircraft zero-zero-seven: Kamey will engage and attempt to force contact to surface; standby."

"Zero-zero-seven standing by."

"Weapons-Bridge: Standby to drop grenades."

Kamey: "Aircraft zero-zero-seven, ready to launch torpedoes on your command."

"Aircraft zero-zero-seven, let's hope it doesn't come

to that."

K-153

"It is time to load the SS-N-5 into the launcher Comrade Captain," the P O ordered.

"Nyet!" Captain Second Rank Ivan Mayakovsky vetoed the suggestion. "Antennas are up. We wait for final instructions from Moscow."

"Captain Mayakovsky, we are under attack by an American destroyer. We must defend ourselves. The orders clearly state that we are to avoid detection at all costs and the SS-N-5 is to be lunched on my command."

"We wait for further orders," the Captain said stubbornly. "We wait."

Several tense minutes of threats from the Political Officer was suddenly interrupted by the communications officer.

"Comrade Captain, urgent message from Moscow."

Mayakovsky quickly grabbed the flimsy sheet of paper from the communications officer and breathed a sigh of relief.

"We do not launch the missile," he said to the Political Officer, handing him the message.

Captain Second Rank Ivan Mayakovsky
Commanding Officer Submarine K-153
Tensions between the Soviet Union and the United States have reached a peaceful conclusion. All Soviet naval

*vessels deployed as part of Operation Anadyr are to
cease operations immediately and return to base.
Fleet Admiral Sergei Gorshkov
Commander in Chief*

"Comrade Kolyada," Mayakovsky said to his second in command, "Dive to 300 feet, rig the ship for silence. Down periscope."

Stepping back as the periscope retracted into its housing, Captain Mayakovsky turned to the navigator, "Warrant Officer Volkov set a course for Polyarni Submarine Base."

****

USS Kamey

SO1 Jack Reed had been carefully monitoring the PING, PING, PING, of sonar echo returns from *K-153* when the sound and the blimp on the screen suddenly disappeared.

"I've lost him sir," Reed told the CIC Officer, frantically twisting dials on the sonar console in a vain attempt to regain contact.

"Lost him? "I thought we had a positive fix on him," exclaimed Ensign Edward Jones, the Combat Information Officer.

"We did, Sir, one minute he was there, the next he was gone... just disappeared."

"Bridge-Sonar: We've lost contact with the submarine."

"CIC-Bridge: check with aircraft zero-zero-seven. See if he still has contact.

"*Kamey:* Aircraft zero-zero-seven: We've lost contact too. I'm getting low on fuel, request permission to return to base."

"Permission granted zero-zero-seven. Thanks for your help."

****

Washington, The Oval Office

As darkness and a cold, blustery chill settled over the Nation's Capitol President Kennedy and his closest advisors were clearly being warmed by the latest communication from Premier Khrushchev.

All missiles and their launching facilities in Cuba would be removed. Despite Khrushchev's pledge, however, quarantine operations would remain in effect while the final curtain was slowly being drawn on negotiations for removal of the IL-28 bombers also based in Cuba. The major obstacle to the removal of the medium-range bombers came from Castro, who was insisting that Cuba had been betrayed by Khrushchev and the Soviet Union. After several days of behind the scenes negotiations between the Kremlin and Havana and assurances by Khrushchev that America would not invade Cuba, Castro finally agreed to the removal of the bombers.

The "standoff in the Caribbean," which had brought the world to the brink of nuclear war was effectively over, but not everyone in Washington, particularly some of the top Pentagon brass, were happy with the outcome.

"Damn it," fumed General LeMay "we had the Russians on the run. We were about to kick their commie butts and they knew it," the General complained to Secretary McNamara.

"Yes General, we probably could have kicked some ass, but at what price? Had we not compromised, we can be assured that the price to the United States, indeed the world, would have been indescribable."

"There is no question," the National Security Advisor interjected, "that we've been severely tested and having come so close to the edge, we must make it our business not to ever pass this way again."

"Be that as it may, Mr. President," General LeMay growled, "but in my opinion, this is the greatest defeat in our history."

The compromise was a particularly sharp embarrassment for the Soviet Union because the withdrawal of U.S. missiles from Italy and Turkey were a secret deal between President Kennedy and Premier Khrushchev.

Although most Americas didn't know it, Thanksgiving 1962 had arrived early. A fact that thousands of American service men, particularly the Sailors and Marines serving aboard a variety of naval warships a mere 90 or so miles off the coast of Florida would never forget.

Chapter 12

November 20, 1962

After five long weeks, filled with uncertainty, fear and stress, the quarantine was lifted and all Atlantic Fleet ships were directed to return to their home ports.

USS Kamey

Having lost contact with *K-153, USS Kamey* continued to search until a message transmitted from a P-3 Orion long-range anti-submarine aircraft reported sighting the submarine on the surface 200 miles northeast of the quarantine zone.

Suddenly the men of *USS Kamey* found themselves once again engaged in the mundane activities of getting the ship spruced up for entering port. Considering the destroyer's seven month Mediterranean deployment just prior to getting underway for the current crisis, the aging destroyer had been deployed for more than 250 days.

The swabbing, chipping paint, shining brass and general bitching was gratefully interrupted by the ear-piercing trill of the boatswain's pipe.

"How hear this! Now hear this! This is the Captain speaking. At 1800 today, the President formally declared an end to the naval quarantine of Cuban. The Commander-in-Chief, Atlantic Fleet has directed that all Atlantic Fleet units return to their home ports and commence normal peacetime operations. *Kamey* will depart the quarantine zone at 2400 and barring any unforeseen operational orders we should be home in time to enjoy Thanksgiving with our families.

"The XO, Lt. Commander Bolton, and I want to personally thank each member of this crew for your outstanding performance of duty. You have clearly demonstrated your willingness to respond quickly to our country's needs when called upon to do so. Commanding the *USS Kamey* during this perilous time in our history, with this remarkable crew will always be one of the most cherished memories of my naval career."

"*Kamey* will continue to provide plane guard services for *USS Lexington* during flight operations tomorrow. At the conclusion of flight ops at approximately 1300 tomorrow afternoon, *Lexington* will continue on to Naval Air Station Pensacola, where she will assume a new role as a training carrier and *Kamey* will return to Mayport.

"Thank you again, one and all, for a truly outstanding job."

"What's a training carrier?" Ensign Harris asked Chief Curtis.

"That's a carrier that has pretty much outlived its usefulness as a fleet carrier," the chief answered. "Its sole purpose is to provide a practice landing deck for flight students. I believe it is the final stage of flight training before flight students get their wings."

"Hummm; I never knew that. Come to think of it, though, it does makes sense, you sure wouldn't want a bunch of wannabe flyboys trying to land an airplane onboard a capitol warship of the line now would we?"

"Ah… no, Sir, can't say that we would, and that's why the Navy it all of its great wisdom has designated an older carrier to be used as a training carrier."

"How many training carriers does the Navy have," the young junior officer asked.

"Just one: the *Antietam,* an *Essex*-class carrier, like *Lexington,* built near the end of World War II. She was a frontline carrier during the Korean War and for the past five years has served as the Navy's training carrier."

"So why is *Antietam* being replaced?"

"I don't know for sure but, if I had to guess, she's probably in bad need of a major overhaul. Naval aircraft, including trainers, have gotten bigger and heavier and without a long, expensive overhaul to lengthen and reinforce her flight deck I seriously doubt that *Antietam* is able to handle them.

"If *Lexington* is an *Essex*-class carrier wouldn't the same logic apply to it?"

"No not really. *Lexington* has gone through several renovations since Korea and was actually finishing up a major yard period to prepare her for this training task when
this thing started. Replacing *Antietam* with *Lexington*,
which will probably be around for another 20-25 years,
will save the taxpayer a whole seabag full of money.
And, as a training carrier, *Lexington*, won't count against
the number of carriers the Navy is allowed under international agreements."

"Well I'll be dammed. Thanks for the education, Chief.
Now I know what they meant at the academy when they
told us 'Chiefs run the Navy.' "

"Well, now that's not entirely true, Mr. Harris. The
chiefs' job is to make sure officers know what they are
doing," Chief Curtis laughed. "As sure as day turns to
night, when a new junior officer comes aboard, it's only
a matter of time until he starts to tell the men of his department or division, how do to their jobs. It's the chief's
responsible to make sure that officer knows what he is
talking about."

"If you say so, Chief. As a lowly ensign I'm sure not going to dispute what the Chief, says," Ensign Harris
smiled. "Catch you later; I want to grab a bite to eat before going on watch."

****

USS Lexington

As the last S2F, piloted by Lieutenant Commander Tex Atkinson, snagged the number two wire for a perfect landing the *Lexington* commanding officer Captain L.C. Powell turned to the executive officer and said: "Secure from flight ops, and have *Kamey* come alongside to top off her tanks."

Following the refueling, Captain Powell came on the ship-to-ship phone and spoke with Captain Feeney.

"Captain, on behalf of the ship's company and air group personnel, I want to thank you and your crew for an outstanding job while performing ASW and plane guard duties for the Lady Lex. As a small token of our appreciation, the supply officer is sending *Kamey*, via highline, 25 gallons of ice cream. Kamey is hereby released to return to her homeport and I look forward to working with you and your fine crew again."

Captain Feeney was smiling from ear to ear as he acknowledged the aircraft carrier skipper's comments and generosity.

"Thank you, Sir. It has been a pleasure working with *Lexington* and you can rest assured your generous gift is greatly appreciated and will be a wonderful enhancement to the evening meal. As far as working with *Lexington* in the future, regrettably that's probably not going to happen. *Kamey* is scheduled for decommissioning in mid-January."

With that final announcement Commander Ralph Feeney, *USS Kamey's* fourteenth and final commanding officer, stood at attention and saluted as his proud old greyhound pulled away from the Navy's newest training carrier and set a course for Naval Station, Mayport, Florida.

****

Naval Station Mayport, Florida

The late autumn sky was a deep blue, with a sprinkling of white fluffy clouds as the crew of the *USS Kamey,* decked out in their dress blues, carried out the centuries old tradition of "manning the rail" for entering port. A gentle breeze blowing from shore carried the sounds of music performed by a detachment of the Navy Band and several high school bands, to the ears of delighted *Kamey* crewmembers — a sure sign that the aging warship had returned home from the sea. Through his binoculars Captain Feeney was astonished at the size of the welcoming party shouting and waving from the crowded pier.

"Damn! It looks like half of Duval County is waiting for us," the Captain said, passing the binoculars to his executive officer.

"You got that right," Lt. Commander. Bolton, his mouth slightly ajar, said. "I can't imagine what it's going be like when the *Shangri-La* gets back."

The Mayport-based ASW carrier *Shangri-La* and several other larger ships, particularly those with photo capabilities would remain on station to provide photographic surveillance of Soviet merchant ships removing missiles and aircraft from Cuba for several more days.

"Let's get ready to take her alongside, Paul," Feeney replied. "Boatswain, set the sea and anchor detail."

Standing in the first rank of the R Division formation on the helicopter deck, SF2 Andy Warden sniffed the air several times.

"Smell that boys?" he said in a low tone still standing at parade rest and staring straight ahead as the distance between the ship and pier steadily decreased. "That's the golden smell of beer. I bet old Marty is sitting them up right now."

Warden was legendary throughout the destroyer Navy for his ability to sniff out the nearest beer joint in any port in the world. Though he had his skeptics, few could deny that he was right seventy-five percent of the time.

Within minutes the yelling and shouting of family members and well wishers could easily be heard as the tugs eased *USS Kamey* alongside the pier. As soon as the first line was made secure the 1mc came to life.

"Now shift colors. Liberty will commence for duty sections one and three at 1500 and will expire on board at 0700. All officers and chief petty officers please report to the Wardroom."

"Gentlemen," Captain Feeney said as soon as the last man had found a seat in the officers' mess, "We'll be having a visit from Commander Destroyer Squadron Sixteen tomorrow at 1300. So inform your men before they depart on liberty that there will be a personnel inspection at 1400. There have been a number of leave requests coming across my desk in the last several days but, at the request of the ComDesRon Chief of Staff, there will be no leave granted until after the ComDesRon visit. I'm sorry about that, I know everyone wants to get home as quickly as possible, but the Chief of Staff made it abundantly clear that the Commodore wants everyone who was onboard during our little Caribbean adventure to be on board for this official visit."

****

Atlantic Fleet Mobile Photographic Group
Norfolk, Virginia

Nearly all the photographers of Mobile Photo, including PH2 Ty Stephens, had returned from quarantine coverage and were looking forward to less stressful photo assignments, despite the proud realism that many of their photos and motion picture footage had been published on the front pages of newspapers and shown on television around the world.

But the man most proud of Mobile Photographic Group coverage was a man who hadn't left Norfolk during the entire crisis, Commander Jack Sermons, Commander of the elite Norfolk based Atlantic Fleet Mobile Photographic Group. His photographers, many of whom were only recent graduates of the Navy's prestigious School of Photography at Pensacola, Florida, had documented the crisis around the clock from aircraft, surface ships and submarines. Their photographs and motion picture footage had presented the world with undisputable proof that the Soviet Union had attempted to establish a nuclear missile base on the island of Cuba.

Three days after the President declared an end to the crisis, the Chief of Naval Operations, in a fleet wide message, pointed out that the entire operation had been a magnificent testimonial for America's armed forces particularly the crews of the numerous ships and aircraft taking part in the operation. He further praised senior military commanders and commanding officers whose professional competence, courage, and diplomatic skill allowed them to quickly move large numbers of troops, ships and aircraft into position to carry out a lengthy, tedious, and very sensitive operation.

In recognition of their professionalism, dedication and patriotism the Secretary of the Navy authorized two service medals for Navy and Marine Corps personnel serving in Cuban waters during the Cuban quarantine. The Navy Expeditionary Medal was authorized for service performed between January 3, 1961 and October 23, 1962. The Armed Forces Expeditionary Medal was authorized for service from October 24 through December 31, 1962.

In addition to receiving the Armed Forces Expeditionary Medal PH2 Stephens was also awarded the Navy Achievement Medal and a Letter of Commendation from the commanding officer of the *USS Kamey*.

While other Mobile Photographic Group members were awarded the Navy Expeditionary Medal or the Armed

Forces Expeditionary Medal, Commander Sermons was awarded the Meritorious Service Medal for his performance in ensuring still and motion picture photographers were on hand to document every facet of the Cuban operation.

Gathered on the parade field of Commander–in-Chief Atlantic Fleet Headquarters for an awards ceremony, the Mobile Photographic Group boss, in accepting the Meritorious Service Medal from the Commander-in-Chief Atlantic Fleet, told the admiral and the hundred or so others gathered for the ceremony: "I accept this award on behalf of the finest group of photographers and cameramen to ever pick up a camera … the photographers of Mobile Photo Group Atlantic, who are always ready and willing to go in harm's way to document naval operations. This medal is for them.

****

USS Kamey
Naval Station Mayport, Florida

In typical Florida fashion, the late November tempera-
ture had dropped several degrees from the previous day
and a steady northeasterly breeze made it a tad uncom-
fortable for the crew of the *USS Kamey* as they stood at
parade rest in preparation for the 1400 personnel inspection by Captain Samuel Littlejohn, Commander
Destroyer Squadron Sixteen.

After a few brief remarks of introduction by Captain
Feeney, Commodore Littlejohn, a graying World War
II naval officer, took a position at a lectern in front of
the destroyer's hanger bay door gave a fake shiver then
addressed the crew.

"*USS KAMEY!* At ease. In light of the weather and the
fact that you are all anxious to get on with liberty and
leave I am going to dispense with the customary personnel inspection at events such as this and simply welcome you home and tell you how proud I am of this
great ship and every man who has sailed aboard her
since I took command of Destroyer Squadron Sixteen
nine months ago.

"In that period of time you have repeatedly distin-
guished yourself and the United States Navy: First during a long Mediterranean cruise in defense of the United States and most recently as a part of Hunter-Killer
Group Bravo during the Cuban quarantine. I am pleased
to tell you that, on behalf of the President of the United
States, many of you will be receiving the Armed Forces
Expeditionary Medal as well as several Letters of
Commendation for your heroic and unselfish contribu-
tions to your Navy of your country.

"On a personal note, I am extremely proud of you and offer my grateful appreciation for your fine work, long hours, patience, and perseverance. Well done."

"ATTENTION!" Lt. Commander Bolton yelled as the commodore saluted, stepped away from the lectern and walked inside the tiny hanger bay. The crew continued to stand at attention until the OOD announced "ComDesRon Sixteen departing."

A few moments later, after escorting ComDesRon-Sixteen off the ship, Captain Feeney returned to the hanger deck and walked to the lectern.

"I would like to add a final comment to the attaboys expressed by the commodore and say once again how proud I am to have served as your commanding officer. You have served your country, your Navy and your ship with great courage and dedication and for that I salute you.

"XO, take charge and dismiss the ship's company."

"Aye, Aye Sir." Bolton responded. "Boatswain pipe liberty call."

"Department Heads take charge and dismiss your men."

****

[144]

Chapter 13

Charleston Navy Shipyard
Charleston, South Carolina
March 11, 1963

For what should have been a normal workday at the busy South Carolina Naval Shipyard, most shipyard workers and the crew of the *USS Kamey* — all 50 of the remaining ship's compliant of 350 — were laid back enjoying the warmth of a beautiful early spring day and discussing the previous week's events. The most talked about subject amongst the enlisted men aboard the 19-year-old warship was the release of two new Beatles records "From Me to You" and "Thank You Girl." For the sports enthusiasts it was Pete Rose making his Cincinnati Reds debut with two hits against the Chicago White Sox in his first two at bats in spring training; and the 70 points Wilt Chamberlain of the San Francisco Warriors scored against the Syracuse Nationals.

In the wardroom the talk among the few remaining officers centered about the pending 1300 decommissioning ceremony and recent reports of a military coup in Syria and a diplomatic break in relations between Somalia and Great Britain.

"I've said it before and I'll say it again," Lt. Commander Bolton said, angrily slamming a copy of the *Charles-*

ton Courier down on the table. "The world is going to hell in a hand basket and nobody in Washington seems to give a shit."

"What's the problem, XO?" Lieutenant Jack Winslow, *Kamey's* third ranking officer asked.

"What's the problem? Have you read this," Bolton said pointing to the newspaper's headline story. "Relations between governments all over the world are falling apart and you can bet your sweet ass the good old U. S. of A is going to be called upon to take care of it. When I read crap like this I'm damn glad that I'm retiring. Let somebody else fight the world's battles for them. I'm damn tired."

"I don't think I've ever seen the XO rant like that over politics before," Lt. (jg) Charlie Slack whispered to Ensign John Miller.

"Don't pay it no mind," the personnel officer replied, "the XO has spent most of his life in the Navy and it all comes to an end today. Can you imagine what it must feel like to basically leave the only job you've ever had after more than 30 years?"

"I guess you're right. It's gotta be pretty emotional," commented Slack. "What about you John, you sticking around for thirty."

"Nope, don't think so. I'm grateful for the Navy ROTC scholarship that put me through collage but as soon as my four-year commitment is up, I'm finished. I want to go to law school."

"Well in just a few more hours we'll all bid the old *USS Kamey* farewell and move on the next stage of our lives. You have to admit though; life aboard *Kamey* has been anything but dull. She's been a good ship. I think I'm actually going to miss her," Ensign Harris joined in.

Seabags and other personal items belonging to the crew were being stacked on the pier for easy retrieval upon conclusion of the decommissioning ceremony, their owners trying unsuccessfully to hide their true emotions, joked about how great life was going to be at their new duty station.

"Shore duty!" Petty Officer Andy Warden exclaimed slapping BM2 Donald Patton on the back. "Man you're going to shore duty. No more sea and anchor details, no more piping the brass aboard, you're one lucky bastard, Boats, you know that?"

"Lucky! You call setting around on my ass watching some E-2 swab the decks in a barracks lucky? No man, I joined the Navy to go to sea, not lollygagging around some damn shore station. Sailors belong on ships and ships belong at sea... lucky my ass."

"Well I for one am looking forward to it." RM1 Jeff Nagle said, reading his orders to instructor duty for the umpteenth time. "I think I'm going to enjoy teaching and if I'm any good at it I just might take up teaching as a second career when I get out of the Navy."

The pros and cons of shore duty came to an abrupt end with the warbling of the bosun's pipe.

"Man decommissioning stations. Now man all decommissioning stations."

"Well here we go gents" Patton said, "Let's look sharp out there. This is the last time we'll ever man the rail of the best ship in the Navy."

"I'll drink to that," SF2 Andy Warden said. "I'll surely drink to that."

"Hell, Warden you'll drink to anything," DC3 Frank Anderson laughed as they quickly vacated the R Division berthing quarters for the last time.

****

With the crew in position and speeches by a large assembly of senior naval officers finished, Captain Feeney turned to the Officer of the Day and ordered that Lt. Commander Bolton and BTC Maxwell Dunlap be piped over the side into retirement.

The warbling of the bosun's pipe suddenly seemed sad as an equally sad-sounding voice said:

"Executive Officer, *USS Kamey* departing."

"Chief Boiler Technician, B Division departing."

Pausing on the quarterdeck Lt. Commander Bolton turned to the duty officer, saluted and asked; "Permission to leave the ship." He then faced the stern of the ship, saluted the flag and slowly walked down the gangway.

Seconds later, the exact same performance was repeated by BTC Maxwell Dunlap. As he saluted the flag the crusty old chief lingered for a moment, wiped at the corner of his right eye as he dropped the salute, did a sharp left face and continued down the gangway.

"You alright Max?" Bolton asked his long-time friend and shipmate. "You weren't crying were you?"

"Crying! Hell no. What would I have to cry about? I just got a little stack gas in my eye, that's all."

"Yeah, me too," Bolton sniffled, putting his arm on the chief's shoulder. "Okay old buddy, what say we go to Tennessee and do a little hunting?

Once the two veteran destroyermen had left, Captain Feeney ordered the lowering of the commissioning pennant, which in keeping with tradition, was then presented to the Captain

Looking longingly at the ribbon like red, white and blue pennant. Feeney turned to look at the decommissioning guests seated on the pier and ordered, "Strike the colors."

With those three simple words, the United States destroyer *USS Kamey* ceased to exist as an American man of war and the crew, knowing they had served her well, silently made their way down the gangway, retrieved their seabags and departed the gallant old warship for the last time.

After two decades of faithful naval service the proud "Tin Can" was now but a lifeless gray hulk of metal moored alongside the pier awaiting her final fate.

####

Epilogue

The Cuban Missile Crisis was the closest the world has ever come to nuclear war. The United States Armed Forces were at their highest state of readiness since World War Two; and Soviet field commanders in Cuba were prepared to use battlefield nuclear weapons, courtesy of the Soviet Union, to defend the island if the U.S. invaded. Luckily, thanks to the bravery of two courageous statesmen, U.S. President John F. Kennedy and Soviet Premier Nikita Khrushchev, total disaster was averted.

Fifty years after the clandestine introduction of offensive weapons of mass destruction into Cuba, military and political historians agree that the installation of such weapons would have constituted not only a direct threat to the peace and security of the Western Hemisphere but the entire world and that threat had to be countered quickly and effectively.

During the week of October 15, 1962 the President and his civilian and military advisors canvassed the alternatives open to the United States. The conclusions reached, as announced to the Nation by President Kennedy on October 22, called for a strict quarantine on all offensive military equipment under shipment to Cuba.

All dependents of U.S. military personnel at Guantanamo Bay, Cuba were evacuated to the United States and an intensive air surveillance of the South Atlantic was initiated to keep track of the more than 2,000 commercial ships usually in the area at any given time.

The massive movement of ships, aircraft, and troops, together with their weapons and equipment, was carried out with unprecedented speed. America's military forces were fully ready for their assignment when the President addressed the Nation on Monday evening October 22.

Low altitude reconnaissance flights over Cuba; flown by Photographic Reconnaissance Squadron Sixty-Two (VFP-62) started the next day.

When the Quarantine Proclamation became effective at 10:00 a.m. (EDT) on October 24, air and surface units of the Atlantic Fleet were at their designated stations. Tension increased significantly on October 27, when a U-2 reconnaissance aircraft, piloted by Major Rudolf Anderson, Jr., USAF, was shot down. Major Anderson's body was returned to the United States following the crisis and he was buried with full military honors in South Carolina. Anderson was the first recipient of the Air Force Cross, which was awarded posthumously.

Eleven crew members of three other reconnaissance aircraft from the 55th Strategic Reconnaissance Wing were also killed in crashes between September 27 and November 11, 1962.

The four-week Cuban Missile Crisis which occurred during October-November 1962 was both a major challenge for a variety of fleet units and a vital demonstration of the Navy's ability to meet such challenges successfully.

In accomplishing their task, naval aircraft flew approximately 6,000,000 miles and fleet units steamed approximately 780,000 miles.

During the crisis, Navy photographic units, at sea and in the air, were particularly active — monitoring military activities of Cuban and Soviet forces. A new Navy-developed aerial camera was used by both the Navy and the Air Force in the highly effective photo reconnaissance flights over the island; and the Naval Photographic Interpretation Center in Suitland, Maryland provided processing and photo-interpretation services that were vitally important to the hour-by-hour evaluation of the military buildup.

The Cuban Missile Crisis provided the most demanding test of the Navy's Anti-submarine Warfare (ASW) capabilities since World War II. So far as can be determined, not a single Russian submarine, committed to the Cuban operation, escaped detection and tracking. ASW hunter/killer forces averaged 23 days at sea and processed a total of 2,889 hours of submarine contacts.

The crisis further provided a particularly striking demonstration of the responsiveness of the U.S. Marine Corps. Guantanamo was rapidly reinforced by combat-ready Marine units deploying simultaneously from three different locations. Five thousand Marines, completely equipped and ready to fight, were moved into position by sea and by air in 48 hours to augment the Guantanamo garrison. The Caribbean contingency force normally deployed in the area, landed a battalion by sea. A second battalion was airlifted from Cherry Point, North Carolina employing Navy and Marine transport aircraft. A third battalion was airlifted from Camp Pendleton, California by Military Air Transport Service (MATS) aircraft. Additionally, a Marine expeditionary brigade of more than 10,000 troops embarked from West Coast ports in less than 96 hours and sailed to join the East Coast division/wing team in the Caribbean area.

The rapid and immediate deployment of these combat-ready forces into Guantanamo assured the defense of that key Caribbean naval facility.

One hundred and eighty-three ships, 29 aircraft squadrons, a Marine Regimental Landing Team and two Mobile Construction Battalions (Seabees), MCB-4 and MCB-7, took an active part in the Cuban Blockade.

The Cuban Missile Crisis was the key factor in the development of the Hotline Agreement, between Moscow and Washington. The hotline provided a direct communications link between Moscow and Washington which is still in operation today. The purpose of the Hotline Agreement was to provide a direct link so the leaders of the two Cold War countries could communicate directly to resolve a crisis.

Sources:
SecNavInst 1650.1C CH-3.9 November 1966
Naval Historical Center

The shipboard setting for this novel was the destroyer *USS Zellars (DD-777)*. *Zellars* was decommissioned on March 19, 1971 and later sold to the Iranian Navy where it was renamed Babr (DDG-7) on October 12, 1973. The former DD-777 served as part of the Iranian Navy through the 1990s.

USS Zellars DD-777

Made in the USA
Charleston, SC
16 April 2015